real food
for dogs & cats

FREMANTLE
fine independent publishing PRESS

First published in 2008 by

Fremantle Press

25 Quarry Street, Fremantle, Western Australia 6160

(PO Box 158, North Fremantle, Western Australia 6159)

www.fremantlepress.com.au

Reprinted 2010, 2011, 2013

Editor: Janet Blagg

Design and illustrations: Tracey Gibbs

Printed by Everbest Printing Co Ltd, China

National Library of Australia Cataloguing-in-Publication entry

Author: Middle, Clare (Clare Elizabeth), 1956-

Title: Real food for dogs and cats : a practical guide to giving

                your pet a balanced, natural diet / Clare Middle.

ISBN: 9781921361357 (pbk.)

Subjects: Dogs--Nutrition.

                Cats--Nutrition.

                Dogs--Food--Recipes.

                Cats--Food--Recipes.

                Pets--Feeding and feeds.

                Pets--Feeding and feeds--Recipes.

Dewey Number: 636.7084

Government of **Western Australia**
Department of **Culture and the Arts**

lotterywest
supported

Fremantle Press is supported by the State Government through the Departent of Culture and the Arts.

real food for dogs & cats

a practical guide to feeding your
pet a balanced, natural diet

Dr Clare Middle

contents

In memory of my parents
John and Ethel Horner,
specialist librarians,
who instilled in me a love
of independent and
open-minded investigation

how to use this book

Chapters 1–3 are for dog owners and chapters 4–6 are for cat owners, but it would be beneficial for cat owners to also read chapter 3 on the components of a natural diet for dogs, which has much more detailed information relevant to both dogs and cats.

There is a lot of information in this book if you should need it, but reading the first two pages of chapter 3 is a very good summary and almost all you need to know!

the purpose of this book

In twenty-five years as a veterinarian I have explained the principles and benefits of a natural diet to most of my clients as part of their pet's treatment program, and have given out thousands of copies of my brochure *Natural Diet for Dogs and Cats.* Many more have been read or downloaded from my website or passed on by clients to other pet owners.

Over the same time I have had many happy reports from dog and cat owners on the rapid improvements in their pets' behaviour and health problems following the change from commercial processed pet food to a balanced, primarily raw, natural diet. However for many people the brochure did not contain enough information, and there were still many questions left unanswered.

So here is the book you asked for.

This book provides

dog and cat owners with what may be the most important healing tool for the animals under their care — an understanding of the physiological basis for a natural diet as close as possible to the diet for which nature equipped them and the simple steps to achieve this.

We are increasingly discovering that fresher, more natural whole food is important for our own long-term health. Similarly, feeding your animals the diet nature intended is likely to be the best way of keeping them happy and healthy. And as an added bonus, it is more economical than a premium quality commercial dried dog or cat food diet.

Clare Middle
BVMS, CVA, Cert IAVH
June 2008

foreword

The widespread introduction of grain-based, cooked and processed pet foods which followed the Great Depression of the 1930s, ushered in two co-dependent eras; the era of artificial foods for companion animals and the era of modern companion animal medicine and surgery.

The convenience of processed pet foods has, since the 1930s, allowed companion animal numbers to rise dramatically; however, it has done so at enormous cost. Cooked and processed pet foods have brought with them an alarming escalation in complex medical and surgical problems, including hip and elbow dysplasia. Modern convenience foods provide the ideal biochemical and physiological milieu for the development of a whole range of degenerative conditions veterinarians treat daily and, unfortunately, these processed foods, based principally on carbohydrates, continue today as the mainstay of modern companion animal nutrition.

The animals forced to eat these foods become increasingly plagued by problems such as arthritis, inflammatory bowel disease, epilepsy and cancer. In response to the enormity of these problems, the veterinary profession has developed sophisticated drugs and surgical approaches which rival those used to treat similar human conditions (with disturbingly similar causes).

However, cracks in this now universally accepted approach to companion animal practice (sitting squarely on the foundation of inappropriate nutrition) appeared in the early 1990s with the formalisation of raw feeding for dogs in my book *Give Your Dog a Bone*. This book, aided by the coincidental information explosion of the world-wide web, was the catalyst for a natural feeding movement for companion animals, a movement which gains momentum daily and reveals startling health improvements associated with biologically appropriate nutrition. This approach to health may already outperform much of modern medicine's sophistry.

Dr Middle is among a small number of Australian veterinarians who have since written books validating biologically appropriate nutrition and recommending balanced whole raw foods, and I am delighted by this significant advance within our profession. For those requiring an insight into an approach to raw feeding as presented by an Australian holistic veterinarian, let me recommend this book most strongly.

There can be little doubt that the solution to the health problems assailing modern pets lies ultimately in their return to a more natural diet.

This book will help continue the forward march of balanced, whole, raw foods as the gold standard approach to the health of today's companion animals.

Dr Ian Billinghurst

BVSc (Hons), BScAgr, DipEd

Veterinary surgeon, acupuncturist, and author of:

Give Your Dog a Bone

Grow Your Pups with Bones

The BARF Diet

preface

I have known and worked with Clare since the early 1990s.

Two awkward questions are never far from her lips when she is working: 'Why?' and 'How?'

Like many holistic veterinarians I have spoken with, she has specialised in holistic medicine because too many questions are left unanswered by allopathic (orthodox or Western) medicine. Looking at alternative perspectives on health and adhering to the principle, 'First do no harm,' holistic medicine enables the practitioner to more than double their therapeutic toolbox.

One major difference between current allopathic and holistic perspectives is the perception of health. Allopathically, we tend, with some exceptions, to come in at the end point of a disease process, intervening at the stage where clinical symptoms are present and disease is well established in the body. At this point we are treating hip dysplasia, diabetes, renal disease, cancer, etc. The disease process has a clear head start on therapeutic management.

Holistically, we look at the whole animal and consider any variation from the most optimal condition possible for that individual as an opportunity to intervene early and facilitate balance within the body systems. This early intervention can prevent, postpone or reduce potential health problems.

One of the major tools for balancing any body, regardless of species, is appropriate food. Over the years I have seen animals respond to diet change with loss of 'doggy' smell, itchy skin, and weight, and a corresponding gain of energy, glossy coat, cleaner teeth, greater well being and arguably greater longevity. These are but a few of the benefits.

Clare has done the hard work of looking critically at the natural diet of two of our carnivorous pets, combining this information with scientific knowledge and research, and refining it down to its essential components. To this add 25 years of experience and observation, and you have a basic recipe which can be adapted to individual animals, including the young, the old and the pregnant. Easy steps are presented for changing your animal's diet, partially or completely, to a healthier option.

This book gives you the tools to introduce your dog or cat safely to a natural diet, and to understand 'why' and 'how' your animal can benefit. It will be an invaluable addition to your library that I am sure you will read many times.

Dr Rosemary Hood
BVMS (Hons), BSc, BAppSc (Physio), NAET
Reiki Master, Small Animal Bowen Therapist

introduction

I graduated as a veterinarian in 1979, the first year veterinarians qualified from the newly established Murdoch University in Perth, Western Australia. This was the 1970s, and the age of Aquarius had just dawned! Murdoch was determined to be the best university, a teacher of the new era. We were provided with excellent scientific tuition and were purposefully trained to think laterally by integrating knowledge from differing areas of study.

However, as soon as I graduated, I saw there were gaps in my conventional veterinary training, and I sought wider knowledge to further my ability to treat the animals under my care.

In 1981 I learned basic acupuncture from a short course for veterinarians. Even this limited knowledge allowed me to help many animals that had not responded to the usual veterinary treatments. I also tutored a course at Murdoch University called Environmental Ethics, from which I learned how necessary it was for us to work in harmony with the environment in a scientific way to avoid major health and environmental problems.

When first my daughter and later my son developed respiratory infections which my GP could not cure, I sought the help of a herbalist and a homeopath. Both my children recovered and have never since required antibiotics. Many of my family's subsequent minor health problems I have treated successfully with diet change, homeopathy or herbs.

Having successfully 'experimented' on my family, I decided these treatments must be safe enough for use on animals too, and I wondered why we had not been taught them at university.

In the early 1990s I gained a diploma in homeopathy designed for GPs and dentists; it was the only course at the time available for a vet. Around the same time, I upgraded my acupuncture training to the International Veterinary Acupuncture Society certificate. This training had just become available in Australia, thanks to the efforts of a small group of veterinarians who had formed an acupuncture group as part of the Australian Veterinary Association.

This important step provided the opportunity for vets like me, with an interest in expanding knowledge in alternative veterinary medicine, to meet and work in collaboration. There are now more than 300 Australian and NZ vets trained in acupuncture.

At veterinary conferences and seminars, our lectures and discussions often include debate about the benefits of fresh raw food for pets. Yet the practical physiology of normal nutrition was hardly mentioned when I studied veterinary science, and still is not really taught at veterinary schools. Veterinary students are given very limited information on nutrition, in fact lectures are often sponsored by commercial pet food companies.

Over a period of seventeen years, I worked at, then bought, East Fremantle Veterinary Clinic. I established it as a clinic for integrative therapies (combining natural therapies with the more usual veterinary treatments) for difficult cases that had not responded to normal conventional veterinary treatments or surgery.

Many inspiring and innovative colleagues worked at the clinic — vet nurses and veterinarians who helped me treat and diagnose using homeopathy, acupuncture, herbs, flower essences, Bowen therapy, reiki and kinesiology. We had craniosacral therapists, chiropractors and experienced spiritual healers, and we saw many pets get better and live long lives.

However I still think the single most useful thing an owner can do for their pet is to provide a properly balanced natural diet.

Sometimes the diet alone helps an unhealthy pet; sometimes it contributes to an improvement in the health in conjunction with other therapies. I expect to see a better result with natural therapies in animals that are fed a natural diet.

Three years ago, I sold the clinic to work from a private consulting room. This way of working allows me to treat animals with more time-consuming modalities such as homeopathy and acupuncture, and also allows the time to educate pet owners regarding diet and essential minimum chemical and vaccination use.

Dog and cat breeders and owners in many countries have contributed to the natural diet debate, and the results of a natural diet over many dog and cat generations have been added to the growing pool of 'cause and effect' observations. There is a list of references at the end of this book, and scientific studies are cited throughout, but the truth is that nature is amazingly complex. We still really have only a limited knowledge, and maybe always will have, of all the many and varied interactions that affect absorption and utilisation of food, even in humans.

The research available now in human nutrition shows that a varied diet of fresh vegetables, fruit, whole grains and protein provides our nutritional needs far better than packaged, processed and refined food. Increasingly, governments are encouraging healthy eating, both to improve our health, and to reduce medical and hospital expenditure. The same holds true for our pets: the more fresh and whole the food is, and the more it resembles an animal's natural diet, the more easily the appropriate nutrients in the appropriate combinations will be available.

1
principles of feeding dogs

We need to know a little about how the dog's digestive system works, so that the basic principles of feeding dogs a natural diet will make more sense.

The dog in the wild

The wolf and other wild dogs have been eating raw meat and raw bone for hundreds of thousands of years.[1] Evolutionarily speaking, domestic dogs are not long out of the wild. Their psychology and physiology are adapted to life in the wild and they could, in general, manage well in the wild, either immediately or within a generation or two.

Wild dogs are closely related to our domesticated dogs, in fact dogs can interbreed with wolves. The dog and the wolf were officially recognised and named as the same species, *Canis lupus*, in 1993, under the code of the International Commission of Zoological Nomenclature.[2]

Once we understand the digestive physiology and the basic psychology of dogs in their wild state,[3] the principles of natural feeding will make complete sense.

Dogs are pack animals, not human children
Humans and dogs can form amazing and beautiful bonds. Unfortunately, humans therefore tend to assume that dogs are more similar to themselves than they really are. This anthropomorphisation of our pets can cause significant problems in the feeding and training of dogs.

WARNING: If you anthropomorphise your dog, you may find the material in this book difficult to digest!

The important difference between dogs and humans is that dogs are very hierarchical and therefore seek to know and be sure of their place in the 'dog pack' — that is, your family household.

Fortunately, this crucial fact is becoming better understood, and training methods have improved markedly in the last decade or so, incorporating a more scientific understanding of what the dog is perceiving and feeling.[4] The appropriate feeding of treats provides an enlightening example of this.

You should only ever give a treat when the dog has thoroughly earned it, and never before or during a human meal. Only feed a dog after all the humans in the household have been fed. If the dog is given a treat without earning it, the dog may get a false impression that it is higher than you in the pecking order.

If these rules are not followed, your dog is basically being told by you, in dog language, that they are higher in the household pack order than you are. Dutiful dogs can become over burdened by a sense of responsibility greater than they are capable of managing, making them confused and stressed, and sometimes leading to behaviour problems and even aggression.

As pack animals, dogs tend to copy the traits of the pack leaders to ensure their place in the pack. Therefore your dog will tend to copy your behaviour — whether you feel guilty or undecided, or confident and determined — about a new feeding regime, or anything else!

By law, a dog's behaviour is the responsibility of the owner, and it is important for owners to be aware of this, not only because it can save you expensive fines, but because it can make your dog happier and healthier!

I have seen dogs heal from itchy skin disease, irritable bowel disease, anxious or phobic behaviour and many other unpleasant conditions, simply when owners begin correctly training the dog, because being happier — unstressed — allows the dog's immune system to function better.[5]

The dog's digestive system

In the wild an empty, hungry dog is in peak form to hunt for its next kill. It may be days, even weeks, before the next main meal hops past, but that is fine, as dogs are adapted for this situation.

Dogs are capable of going without a meal for several days — with no loss of energy.

In the wild the next meal cannot be predicted: it is a random event. The dog's digestive system is very different from a human's. Their stomach has evolved to digest food best when it is very full. This means dogs can fill their stomach when they have the chance — after killing a large prey animal — and make the most of the opportunity.

Most digestion of a dog's food occurs in the stomach, which is a highly acidic pH 1–2, primarily due to the presence of hydrochloric acid.[6] This is an extremely corrosive environment, capable of digesting large amounts of raw bone and raw meat.

In contrast, a human stomach is generally about pH 3–4. Human digestion occurs mainly in the intestines, and the stomach functions more like a mixing bowl, combining the food with the enzymes for digestion later in the intestines. Digestive enzymes are very sensitive to the correct pH to do their job well.

Carbohydrates can only be fully digested at a pH of about 4–5, while the optimum environment for starch digestion by the enzyme amylase is pH 6. A dog's stomach rarely or never has such a high pH, because dogs are not meant to be carbohydrate or starch eaters.[7]

Humans eat far more grain and a higher percentage of vegetable matter than dogs, and our digestion favours more continuous eating. We can't digest raw bone at all, or raw meat very well, because our stomachs have too high a pH for this to occur.

Dogs do not chew food well — they have a basic scissor-action jaw which breaks the food into smaller pieces, if at all, prior to swallowing. The thought of gulping down lumps of raw meat and raw bone may sound foreign to us, but that is how dogs are designed to eat! They do not need to chew their food very well like we do, as their stomach acidity does most of that work instead.

The dog's stomach differs from the human stomach in another important way: empty, it is not much larger than the surrounding intestines. However, it is capable of greatly expanding to hold up to 5% of the dog's own total body weight of food.[8] And when the stomach is fully stretched, the glands on the inner stomach wall are stimulated to produce yet more enzymes and hydrochloric acid to aid digestion.

This feedback effect is further boosted by an enzyme called gastrin, which stimulates stomach wall contractions, so that the more full the stomach is, the more contractions occur.

The dog's stomach therefore has to be full and dilated for optimum digestion.

Meals must be principally meat and bone

It is important that the dog's stomach be primarily full of raw meat and raw bone. If a dog's stomach is full of high carbohydrate or starch food which can *only* be fully digested at a pH of 3 to 6, then full digestion is obviously unlikely.

A dog's stomach full of undigested
carbohydrate — and even the premium
brands of dried dog food are generally
30–60% carbohydrate — can lead to
stagnation and bloating, which can be a
life-threatening condition in dogs.

Carnivores are not carbohydrate eaters. For energy
they depend on glucose from non-carbohydrate
sources.[9] Therefore grain, sugar, bread, cakes, pasta,
rice, biscuits and commercial dried dog foods should
therefore generally not be part of a dog's diet.

One cause of bloat[10] is thought to be the gas
produced by bacteria that proliferate in a stomach
environment of about pH 3–6. These harmful
bacteria do not survive well in the low pH stomach

of a dog fed raw meat and bone. Bloat is unlikely to occur in a dog whose stomach has adjusted to a primarily raw meat and bone diet.

Grains and cereals and dried or kibbled dog food, and tinned meat containing cereal, are therefore not good foods to be fed in large quantities to a dog, as they may hinder the correct digestive processes in the dog's stomach. The 3–5% carbohydrate of a balanced natural diet is far more appropriate for dog physiology.

A balanced diet for a dog:
**60–80% raw meat, fat, offal, bone, fish
20–40% vegetables, bran, fruit, herbs,
fish oil, supplements**

When dogs do need carbohydrates
In some cases, small amounts of carbohydrate can be justified if the dog is burning a lot of energy, for example:

- very active working or obedience trial dogs
- young pups growing quickly
- pregnant or lactating dogs
- very thin dogs who do not gain sufficient weight on non-carbohydrate foods
- dogs with digestive system impairment such as exocrine pancreas insufficiency
- dogs who have been on poor quality or high carbohydrate diets for a long time and no

longer have the capacity to adapt to the low
stomach pH needed for raw meat and bone
- very old dogs who are not adapting well to a
  natural diet
- dogs who are unwell and not adapting easily to
  a natural diet.

See pages 90–92 for a full discussion of the best
foods for these special 'high carbohydrate need'
dogs. But note that it would still be unwise to
exceed 10% carbohydrate (by 'wet' weight, that is,
cooked or soaked).

Select carbohydrates from:
- cooked oats, quinoa, barley, millet, dried peas,
  lentils, chick peas, polenta
- cooked sweet potato, swede, turnip, parsnip
- the bran or outer husk of any grain, especially
  oat or rice bran and flax meal.
- Any of these would be far more nutritious than
  commercial dried pet food.

The problem with commercial dried foods

If commercial dried food is used as a carbohydrate
source, include it as no more than about 3% of the
total diet, as it has a lower moisture content than
the fresh foods listed above.

There is no law which enforces the manufacturers
of commercial pet food to provide a full range of

adequate nutrients. Most have a high carbohydrate content to make it profitable to manufacture, as cereal is generally cheaper than protein, and easier to market because it keeps at room temperature, and is convenient for owners to buy, store and handle. Even the best quality commercial dried dog foods can contain 25–60% carbohydrate, on a dry weight basis.

Unfortunately, it is not what nature intended for the dog's digestive system. Also, the grain content should be high quality food rather than the waste by-products or meal contained in many commercial dried foods.

I have found few brands of dried commercial dog food that have an acceptably low carbohydrate percentage of quality grain.[11]

Low carbohydrate studies
Several studies confirm that the development of hip dysplasia in prone dog breeds is significantly reduced if the puppies are raised on a low carbohydrate diet with periods of fasting.[12] The same research has established the benefits of feeding puppies and adult dogs a large proportion of raw bone in their diet.

Raw meat is best
Raw meat contains most essential amino acids, some essential fatty acids, most of the B group vitamins, many trace elements and some antioxidants.

Cooking destroys about 70% of nutrients in raw meat.[13]

Raw bone (and cartilage) not only keeps dogs' teeth healthy and clean, it also contains valuable nutrients including calcium phosphate, collagen and trace minerals. The marrow contains fatty acids and vitamins. Raw bone is nutritious and digestible, so long as it is not too large for the size of dog and if the dog is accustomed to eating raw bone.

Raw fat is beneficial and safe for dogs. It contains essential fatty acids and is the best energy source for dogs. (The full discussion on raw meat, fat and bone begins on page 68.)

Cooking makes bone indigestible and makes fat harmful.

However, generations of some breeds of domesticated dog have long eaten some cooked meat, due to their relationship with humans. And it can be argued that a few dogs with impaired digestive ability, whether due to genetics, age, diet or disease, may be better with some cooked meat at some stages in their lives.[14]

If you must cook meat, it is important that you do not also cook the bone or fat:

- Cooked fat can be harmful, possibly causing acute pancreatitis.

- Never feed cooked bone, as it cannot be digested and may cause blockages or injury to the intestines.
- Remove the fat before cooking the meat.
- Cooking can change the nutrients in fats and oils from useful into harmful ones, so any oil additives should be cold pressed and added unheated.
- Supplements such as fish oil, kelp, flax meal and alfalfa must be added uncooked or unheated.

Fast your dog at least once a week

It is characteristic of the dog's digestive process that the dog thrives best on the whole digestive tract being completely empty at regular intervals.

An empty gut allows the liver to complete its metabolic processes fully, which can only happen when the rest of the digestive tract is totally empty.[15] It takes between about eighteen and thirty hours for the dog's stomach, intestines and bowel to empty.

It is only then — when the blood glucose has dropped beneath a certain level and there is no other source of energy — that the liver is forced to convert glycogen from fat and muscle, and from the liver itself, into glucose for energy.[16] This process is accompanied by the maximum release of pesticides, toxins and other harmful chemicals or drugs from the liver.

The liver is an important organ and its healthy functioning can reduce the incidence of allergy, infection, autoimmunity and cancer.[17]

Toxic chemicals may have accumulated in the liver over many years, from many sources — digested from food or absorbed through the lungs or skin — and may include household cleaning products, white ant and other insect or weed sprays, flea products, mercury from vaccination, exhaust fumes, and pesticides from vegetables, fruit and grain hulls.[18]

Liver detoxification will never occur completely if the dog is fed twice or more a day, seven days a week, week after week. More than six meals a week may compromise the liver's ability to ever fully detoxify.[19]

I recommend you introduce a fasting day when your puppy is about six months old and is down to one meal a day.

Fasting enhances performance

Not only does the liver totally cleanse the body of toxins, it burns excess fat, so the dog can hunt even more effectively. Its senses are also more acute when detoxified.

In the wild a dog with an empty stomach is in peak form to hunt for its next kill.

The dog's use of glycogen as a fuel is an amazingly efficient process. A dog can go for days without food, working hard physically and mentally, in order to find prey.

For this reason, emergency search and rescue dog handlers fast their dogs as soon as a missing person is reported. They know the dogs will be more energetic and work more effectively if they have not been fed for a day or two.[20] Similarly, many dog trainers fast a dog to enhance the effectiveness of their training program, and many owners of racing greyhounds fast their dogs so they can run more quickly.

Exercising your dog on its fasting day is a very good idea, because exercise will then add to the cleansing effect of the fast.

Fasting is not cruel

I have heard owners say they are afraid that if they fast their dog once a week, the dog will be miserable and hate them.

This is an example of looking at a dog's emotions in human terms: the owner is assuming (incorrectly) that not only is it not right for a dog to fast, but that the dog will rationalise in an intellectual way like a human.

It is not cruel to feed a dog only once every one or two days. It may be cruel to feed a dog twice daily, especially with a high carbohydrate meal, as it will never feel completely satisfied because full liver metabolism has not been achieved.

It might, however, be cruel to fast a dog that was on a diet of mainly commercial dried food. It is the combination of fasting with a raw meat diet that is important.

There are also situations when fasting is not beneficial, such as in late pregnancy, puppyhood, and for animals with diabetes.

If, however, you are not happy fasting your dog, it will still benefit from being on a natural diet. It is important for you to feel happy about your choice, as your pet will detect your confidence and respond accordingly.

Feed your dog at random times

It is difficult for some people to accept the idea of feeding a dog only five to six times a week, as it is so different from the daily routine humans tend to follow. Equally counterintuitive may be the notion that it is psychologically and physiologically beneficial to feed your dog at random times.

In the wild, the arrival of food can never be predicted: it is a random event.

Dog trainers are well aware of the principle of random reward:[21] the dog is always alert and ready to earn rewards (or meals), and is pleased when it gets one, but training effectiveness is not reliant on a food reward every time the dog behaves well.

If you feed at the same time each day, the dog will automatically respond like 'Pavlov's Dog' and expect to be fed. This is a conditioned or stress-association response, and precisely what we do not want just prior to feeding, as the stress release of adrenalin reduces blood flow to the upper gastrointestinal tract and reduces effective digestion.

It will be much easier to get your dog to feed randomly if you have had it on a natural diet as a puppy.

Introduce random meal times gradually to puppies. Decrease the number of daily meals to once daily feeding, then include a fast day by the time the puppy is about six months old.

Some owners and dogs will not adapt readily to fewer meals, so move slowly into the new program to find the right level for you and your dog. See page 56 for some ideas to help you change over to random feeding.

A sample feeding program
Here is just one example of a weekly feeding

program, where the dog is fed five meals in the week. You could use the same timetable for the next week, or vary it.

Day 1 — 9am
Day 2 — noon
Day 3 — 7pm
Day 4 — fast
Day 5 — 3pm
Day 6 — 8pm
Day 7 — fast

Note that this feeding regime is for dogs fed a primarily raw meat and bone diet, with no more than 3–5% carbohydrate in each meal. It would not be suitable if the dog ate a diet of primarily commercial dried food.

If random feeding does not work out for you and your dog, that is all right. Simply feeding a natural diet will greatly benefit your pet's health.

Feed by percentage body weight
You should feed approximately 20–30% of the dog's body weight a week — about 2–5% of the dog's body weight in food at each meal, assuming the dog is fed six to seven meals a week.

Growing puppies usually need at
5% of their body weight daily

Fine-tune the amount by deciding whether your dog needs to lose weight or gain it.

Is my dog too fat or too thin?
The best way to tell if your dog is the correct weight is to see if you can easily count six ribs while running your hand over the side of its ribcage.

If you can't easily count that many (or any!) ribs, the dog is too fat, so feed 10% less raw meat and check again in about a month.

If you can feel more than six ribs (or all 13!), then the dog is too thin. Feed 10% more raw meat and check again in about a month.

The smaller the dog, the closer to 5% of its body weight should be fed per meal. This percentage could even be higher in very high energy requiring individuals such as lactating bitches and puppies. Larger dogs generally require the lower end of the range, closer to 3% of their body weight daily.

- A 5kg dog may eat 30% of its body weight weekly, or 1.5 kg.
  If 7 meals a week are fed, each meal weighs about 210g.
  If 6 meals, each meal weighs about 250g
  If 5 meals, each meal weighs about 300g
- A 25kg dog may eat 25% of its body weight weekly, or 6.25 kg. if 6 meals a week are fed, each meal weighs about 850g.
  If 6 meals, each meal weighs about 1 kg.
  If 5 meals, each meal weighs about 1.25 kg.
- A 40kg dog may eat 20% of its body weight weekly, or 8 kg.
  If 7 meals a week are fed, each meal weighs about 1 kg.
  If 6 meals, each meal weighs about 1.3 kg.
  If 5 meals, each meal weighs about 1.6 kg.

Feed until full

To best mirror the wild situation for which their digestive system is adapted, dogs depend on us feeding them a stomach full of raw meat and raw bones (and fish/fish oil, vegetables and herbs of course).

Dogs have no digestive enzymes released in their mouth: the stomach is the major digestion organ, and it has to be well stretched for the optimal release of digestive enzymes to occur.[22] This means that ideally the dog should be fed until it is quite full.

A dog's intestine is really just for absorbing the already digested food, so it is crucial to get correct digestion happening in its stomach.

Those dogs fed on too high a carbohydrate diet may continually be asking for food because they 'know' there is something not right with their feeding situation (and they are correct). If they are always fed in response to their begging, they will never have the chance to complete their liver metabolism, since this requires the intestines to be empty.

Of course you must not feed a dog full with dried dog food or processed or tinned dog food, pasta, rice, or anything other than predominately raw meat and raw bones, otherwise the dog may suffer bloat. (See pages 26–29.)

Do not leave food out constantly

Random feeding is not 'ad hoc' feeding. Optimal digestion for a dog occurs with a small number of large meals.

It is rarely a good idea to leave food out for dogs to help themselves when they feel like it. With a constant supply of glucose from graze feeding, the liver will not produce energy from glycogen stores, or fulfil its important function of clearing harmful chemicals stored in the body.

Also, if you stop providing continuous food for your dog, you will be able to use

mealtimes and the occasional well-timed
treat to train your dog more effectively.[23]

Treats, when used appropriately, can be useful
training aids.[24] Tiny pieces can be given to minimise
the food intake of the dog between meals, while
still helping with training. Dogs must earn a treat,
and it must be a 'chance' event, so the dog does
not expect a treat at the same time every day,
irrespective of it being earned.

Feed according to the season

Nature changes with the seasons, so it is fine to
change the diet from time to time, just as it is natural
for the dog's weight to alter from time to time.
When it comes to the non-meat components of the
diet, it is better to eat whatever food is in season —
it will be more nutritious and economical than food
that is out of season.

Having observed thousands of sick animals over
many years of practice, I agree with the ancient
Chinese position that certain diseases are more
likely to present in particular weather conditions,
and that different foods can help address these
tendencies to disease.

According to traditional Chinese medicine,[25] it
is better to feed 'cooling' foods in summer — raw
vegetables, salad and fruit, especially melon. In
winter, it is better to feed 'warming' foods such

as ginger and cooked vegetables. Following these principles may help relieve ear infections in hot humid weather, heat stress in hot weather, bladder infections with the onset of wet weather, painful backs and joints in winter, and so on.

It also helps to feed raw or cooling foods to animals who feel the heat badly, and more cooked or warming foods to those sensitive to the cold.[26]

Your dog is happy: you are happy

Feeding your dog should become part of your usual routine, not a chore. Relax and enjoy it. Not only are there many advantages to feeding your dog a natural diet no more than once a day, at random times, and with fasting days — there are considerable advantages to you too:

- You will be preparing fewer meals for your dog.
- You can use vegetables and fruits you have readily to hand.
- You won't need to watch the clock for dog feeding time or worry about getting home late because the dog hasn't been fed.
- Your dog will stop begging for treats.
- Your dog will feel satisfied and will not be hungry most of the time.
- Your dog will produce less than half the amount of faeces for you to clean up from the garden.

- You can go away for a weekend and leave the dog with water only (and supervision and company) — relax and imagine all that liver cleansing!

Regardless of the number of meals per week and time of feeding, all dogs on a natural diet reap the ultimate benefit — increased health and happiness.

2
the changeover process for dogs

The Changeover Process for Dogs

Changing a dog from a diet of mainly tinned or cooked meat, processed 'dog roll' or dried dog food, to a natural diet of primarily raw meat and raw bones, maybe also with fasting and random feeding, should be carried out over a three to four week period. Of course, some dogs will take a shorter or longer time to convert than this.

If, after four weeks of trying to change to random feeding times, it still feels better to feed at the same time each day, then that is fine. You and your dog may miss some of the advantages of irregular feeding, but your dog's health will still be much improved simply by the change from processed to natural food.

Many of my clients have returned after a week saying that their dog loves the new diet, has completely converted to it with no problems, and is already happier and healthier for it.

However for some dogs it will take longer to reduce their stomach pH, stretch their stomach or detoxify their liver, or for their lower bowel to learn to deal with a different consistency of gut contents.

Dogs who are older, who have had health problems, or who have been fed a primarily dried commercial food diet, are likely to take the longest to convert.

Some dogs may never be able to convert, or totally convert, to a natural diet, because they are unable to regain the capacity to fully digest properly.

Some authors and breeders believe that Chihuahuas cannot manage on less than two meals a day, and cannot be starved, due to a lack of glycogen metabolism in the liver. However I have met some individuals of this breed that have coped well with once daily feeding.

I have many small breed dog patients who had poor appetites with once or twice daily feeding with processed or cooked food. When converted to a meal of raw food no more than once a day, they came to love their food and their general health improved also.

It is important to go carefully with changing your dog's diet and to do what suits them best as individuals.

I honour the dog's own decision about its diet, and in general, after three to four weeks, if there are foods or herbs the dog repeatedly rejects, then I assume that these foods are not right for the dog.

The nutrients may be present in the diet already, and are not further needed, or for some other reason the dog has decided they are not appropriate.

The Chinese medicine theory that certain foods are beneficial to some individuals but not others may explain why some dogs will not accept certain foods.[27] I would therefore not force a dog to eat any food that is repeatedly rejected over the trial period.

Handling raw meat safely

In the changeover period, there are also adjustments for you to make. If you have not handled raw meat before, there are certain precautions you need to make for the health of the humans in your household.[28]

> Wash the boards and knives used to prepare raw meat (especially chicken) before they are used for handling human foods that will not be cooked.

Approximately 80% of raw chicken (and to a lesser extent other meats) in supermarkets contains *Salmonella* and *E. Coli* bacteria. This has always been the case, and the reason we don't get food poisoning from these pathogens is that we cook the meat. Also, most of us would have built up a degree of resistance (antibodies) to these bacteria due to repeated exposure.

Normal healthy dogs are also immune to these food poisoning organisms. They do not get food poisoning from *Salmonella* or *E. Coli*.[29] Dogs lick their (and other dogs') bottoms, they dig up putrid bones in the garden and they eat other dogs' and cats' faeces, all of which can contain these bacteria, and suffer no ill effects.

If your dog has never had raw meat in its life, and little contact with other dogs, it might not have developed immunity to *E. Coli* and *Salmonella*. If so, the gradual introduction to raw meat over three or four weeks is likely to confer immunity in an otherwise healthy dog. However, I would not make rapid changes to the diet of a very sick or immune-compromised animal if it had never had raw meat before.

Dogs fed raw meat have more bacteria in their faeces than dogs fed commercial food, but this difference need not cause concern.[30] Children exposed to bacteria are healthier than children brought up in clean environments, and households with pets have about 10% less medical expenditure than families without pets. Children brought up on farms have lower rates of skin allergy, asthma and infections. Exposure to naturally occurring bacteria from dogs is more likely to be a source of health in humans than of illness.[31]

Learning to digest raw bone

If the dog's stomach is slow to change to a lower pH, raw bone may be vomited, or appear in the stools not fully digested, but normally this phase is over within a month or so.

If there is undigested bone in the stools for longer than a month, suspect that the bone is too hard — large beef 'marrow' bones often are (see below for the appropriate bone size). Otherwise the dog may have an inability of the pancreas to produce digestive enzymes, so seek veterinary help.

NEVER feed cooked bone. It cannot be digested.

Some dogs have too few teeth to chew bone. These, and dogs with poor jaw or head conformation, such as Schitzus and Chihuahuas, or with uneven healing of skull or jaw fractures following injury, may need their raw bones ground or minced (see pages 73–76).

Bone Size
Some dogs are so keen to consume real food for the first time that they may gulp whole bones down without chewing them. This generally does not cause any problems. However, when the bones are chewed several times, the teeth will get the cleaning benefit, and the bone will have a bit more surface area for more optimum digestion of nutrient.

It is possible (though unlikely) for a bone to get stuck in the back of the mouth or in the oesophagus, so it is advisable to watch your dog carefully when you introduce a new type or size of bone to make sure it chews the bone sufficiently before swallowing. Chicken and turkey necks, for instance, have a slight bend to them and can lodge in the curve of a small dog's oesophagus. This is unlikely to be life threatening, but can be unpleasant to remove.

It is also good psychologically for a dog to chew on, rather than just swallow, raw meat and bone.

Strong chewing activity increases serotonin and endorphin levels in the brain, making the dog feel happy that it has hunted, gathered and killed its prey.

The dog will be happier, and probably better behaved, as these high serotonin and endorphin levels in turn reduce the production of adrenalin or stress hormones, which in turn improves digestion, as too much adrenalin reduces blood supply to the upper gut.

These endocrine feedback mechanisms positively affect all the digestive organs — stomach, intestines, pancreas, liver and adrenals, pituitary gland and thymus.[32] The whole system becomes healthier and better balanced in its functions, all from the dog chewing on raw bone!

Some changeover ideas
WEEK ONE
- In the first week of changing over to a natural diet, try out some different cuts of raw meat and bone to see which your pet likes and can chew easily (chewing several times before swallowing). Small bones are chicken necks, lamb or pork neck, transverse sections at neck or tail, or raw whitebait fish. Medium bones are chicken or turkey necks, whole lamb necks, chicken or turkey wings, lamb shanks, ox or roo tails. Large bones are brisket bones, mutton or goat shanks, venison bones.
- Add different cooked or raw vegetables or fruit and make a list to put on the fridge door of what the pet likes as a reminder.
- Add one piece of raw meat and bone and a vegetable or fruit to each meal for a few days until you are confident to add more.

WEEK TWO
- If your pet is happy with this and shows no excessive detox symptoms, in the second week

at each meal feed half the original food and half the new fresh food.

WEEK THREE

- If your pet is happy with this, then during the third week, feed three quarters of your pet's food the new fresh diet, a quarter the original commercial food.

WEEK FOUR

- During the fourth week, feed only the new natural diet, and amend your list on the fridge regarding which foods do not or do suit your pet — for the benefit of other household members and to jog your memory in the future.

Puppies and pregnant or lactating bitches

For young puppies (three to sixteen weeks) and pregnant or lactating bitches, a higher than normal calcium and energy requirement is needed, and ground raw bone may be the best alternative to whole raw bone. This is especially so if the mother dog has a poor appetite and gets full easily, or is too preoccupied with her puppies to chew bone or eat properly.

Wolf puppies up to about three or four months are given regurgitated partly digested bone by adult wolves: mincing or grinding the bone is the closest we can get to this.[33]

You can mince your own raw bone with a suitable food processor or grinder. Add much needed calcium in the form of raw bone in ground or minced form in the early days of eating, which is from about three weeks of age until whenever they are capable of chewing whole bone.

There are some good pre-made raw meat and bone patties available which have oils, herbs and vegetables already added which are ideal to start young puppies on, if they are not the best bone chewers in the early stages.

Some very young puppies do not put on weight easily, so may benefit from some whole grain. From 5% to 10% of the total diet of well-cooked oatmeal, pearl barley, split peas, polenta or rolled or ground quinoa or amaranth, will contain far more nutrition than the grain waste by-products of many common premium commercial dried pet foods.

It is essential for young puppies to learn to chew raw bone, for all the health benefits to teeth, jaw development and emotional balance and nutrition, as in adult dogs.

Puppies can be started, under close supervision, with the triangle flap of the chicken wing tip, and, as soon as they are able, a section of chicken or turkey neck, or whatever sized raw bone suits their ability to chew.

Never add dried calcium powder, as it is possible to add to too much calcium in this way.

Use other natural calcium containing foods such as plain low fat yoghurt or cottage cheese if they suit the pup. These and as many raw bones as the pup can eat will provide a balanced and correct calcium level.

Frequency of feeding puppies
- four meals a day for three week to three month old puppies (or from start of weaning)
- three meals a day for three to four month old puppies
- two meals a day for puppies four to six months old
- one meal a day, then slowly introduce a fast day per week over the next month or so, for six month old puppies.

Pregnant and lactating bitches can require up to ten times as much energy as a non-breeding adult dog. As with puppies, their calcium requirement is also high, so they need plenty of raw bone or natural calcium foods but NOT added calcium powder. (When extra calcium is really necessary, the best source is in liquid form, but feeding calcium-rich foods is an effective way to build it up in the animal's system.)

As with pups, it may be easier to pack in the calcium and calories by feeding ground raw meat and bone instead of or as well as whole bones if she has a poor appetite or is losing weight (you should only be able to count six or fewer ribs). If your breeding mum is carrying plenty of weight, then just continue with the normal adult dog diet with plenty of bones and with no grain.

Changing to random feeding

When a dog is fed at exactly the same time each day, this can trigger an adrenalin or stress-association reaction if it is *not* fed at that time. The owner can divert this reaction into a more positive activity like playing, going for a walk, or being rewarded for doing a trick. That way, a positive, healthy association can be created instead of the expectation of being fed at that time, or whenever the owner enters the kitchen, depending on what the triggering association is.

If you constantly walked past your dog's walking lead through the day, it might think it was walk time, just as it may think it is food time when you walk into the kitchen. Most people wouldn't feel compelled to walk their dog several times a day just to ease their guilt, so why feed a dog frequently for that reason?

It may take 2 to 3 weeks for the dog to create a new emotional pattern, but it will be far happier and healthier in the long term.

It is the owner's responsibility as 'pack leader' to initiate and establish healthy patterns. This is thinking like a dog, and it honours your dog.

Liver detoxification

Some pet owners have abandoned feeding their dogs a natural diet when, after a few days, their dog seemed to become unwell, perhaps with diarrhoea or vomiting. However, they very likely misinterpreted these symptoms as indicating that the diet was not good for the dog.

The reverse in fact is true, because these reactions are signs of toxins being excreted, and of the dog's digestive processes adapting to the change in diet.

In general, it will take longer for an older dog to detoxify, and some very old dogs may be too old to take on the challenge — although I have seen many improve dramatically. Old dogs with arthritis can respond very well when raw bone is introduced to their diet.

Depending on the dog and its condition, it can take anything from a few days to several weeks to fully detoxify when changed from a commercial dog food diet to a natural diet, so don't give up too soon!

When converting your dog to a natural diet, the following initial changes may be observed, showing that liver detoxification is occurring:

- diarrhoea
- vomiting
- itchy skin
- hair loss
- lethargy
- irritability
- raw bones not fully digested
- drinking more water than usual
- reduced appetite.

These signs, which generally occur for a day or so, are soon replaced by the following signs of good health:

- no vomiting
- normal stools
- coat in sleek and shiny condition
- no itching
- less hair loss
- a happier more playful dog with more energy
- less irritable or aggressive behaviour
- no visible undigested bone in the stools
- possibly lower liver enzyme and lower cholesterol levels on blood test.

Blood test anomalies during changeover

Some slight but unusual changes may occur with the blood results of dogs fed a natural diet.

Your vet may not be familiar with these, if used to treating dogs fed commercial dog food.

Blood tests taken before the diet change may have shown high liver enzyme levels indicating hyperthyroidism, Cushing's disease or hepatitis due to infection, exposure to pesticide, drug or vaccination reactions.

A change to a natural diet will bring down these high liver enzyme levels due to improved liver function. It can take at least three months for the liver enzyme levels to reduce to normal. In the meantime, they may show an *increase* for a few days or weeks to an even higher level than when the condition was diagnosed prior to the change to a natural diet.

This will be especially noticed in dogs that are also given liver cleansing herbs or homeopathics or acupuncture along with the conversion to a natural diet.

Again, this paradox is due to the detoxification process. The liver is becoming more competent at its job, and may be excreting toxic waste products that have been accumulating all its life.

**The initial increase in liver enzyme level
is almost always accompanied by a big
improvement in the dog's condition — it
is happier, more lively and energetic — and
a corresponding *decrease* of symptoms
such as poor appetite, vomiting, diarrhoea
and weight loss.**

It can be very confusing for vets and dog owners to see this improvement, while the blood test looks worse. But if the dog feels and looks better (and the great majority do), that means it is detoxifying nicely, so keep going, and continue to monitor the blood levels until they return to normal.

Of course, if the dog does not look or feel better, then further investigation is warranted by your vet.

Kidney function levels may also vary slightly when dogs are put on a natural diet. One author found that a naturally fed dog can have a blood urea nitrogen of about 5–10% higher than the range considered normal in veterinary pathology laboratories.[34]

However this change is quite small, so is still likely to be within the normal range, and is probably due to the more effective protein digestion of the dog's stomach. It may also be that 'normal' laboratory levels were ascertained without reference to the dog's diet, and were probably derived from dogs fed mainly or totally dried food diets, which is the case for most laboratory animals used for research.

> Research shows that feeding a high raw
> meat natural diet does not predispose
> to kidney disease. In fact the good
> quality protein may help prevent
> such conditions.[35]

I am often called on to treat 'kidney failure'
dogs (and cats) that have been recommended for
euthanasia. With a natural diet and homeopathic,
herbal and acupuncture treatment, many have lived
normal lives for months or years, with lower blood
urea levels than when diagnosed.

Vaccination

As well as a change to a natural diet, the next
most health-enhancing change for your dog could
be to only vaccinate when necessary. A blood test
can be used to screen for antibody levels to any
infectious diseases in your area, such as parvovirus or
distemper. If sufficient antibodies are present in the
blood, vaccination may not be necessary.

Vaccine producers advise against vaccinating your
dog if it has suffered long-term health problems
such as allergy, arthritis, colitis, low immunity or
autoimmune disease. Excessive vaccination can
overwork the immune system, possibly leading to
further health problems.[36] If that is the case for your
dog, you can relax about not vaccinating routinely if
sufficient antibody is shown from the blood test.

A routine blood test is a good investment in preventative health for your dog. It can be combined with an annual check up with the vet to check teeth, ears, eyes, heart, nails, lymph nodes, anal glands, mammary glands, spine and joints.

In older animals, it can also be used to check the liver, kidneys, blood cells and glucose. This blood test can be taken about every three years if the antibody levels continue to be sufficiently high.[37] You will be practicing excellent preventative medicine, as any problems are likely to be picked up before symptoms show.

Preventative health checks combined with feeding a natural diet, and using only the vaccinations and parasite prevention your dog needs, will likely cost you less over the years, as your dog will be less likely to get sick.[38] The only increased expense may be that you will be buying raw meat and bones, etc, for a greater number of years as your dog is likely to live a longer life!

Further reading

If you feel any confusion about changing your dog over to a natural diet, the following readings (see the bibliography for full details) are recommended:

• The natural feeding sections in *The Complete*

Herbal Handbook for the Dog and Cat by Juliette de Bairacli Levy.

- Dr Ian Billinghurst's *Grow Your Pup with Bones*, *Give Your Dog a Bone* and *The BARF Diet*.
- Mogens Eliasen's *Raw Food For Dogs* has many detailed pages just on feeding puppies and on changing adult dogs over to a natural diet.
- One of my clients, Erica Williams, has recently published a natural diet dog recipe book called *FeedWell*.

3
components of
a natural diet
for dogs

Components of a Natural Diet for Dogs

NOTE: This chapter contains information relevant to both dogs and cats, with an emphasis on a natural diet for dogs. See chapter 6 for a summary of information for cats.

The following pages summarise the information in this chapter so if you only have time to read one or two pages, this has all you need to know! Perhaps you can make a photocopy and stick it on your fridge door as an easy reminder. Soon feeding your pet naturally will become second nature and you will wonder why you ever did it differently.

A dog in the wild would naturally eat whole small animals — the guts of which would contain fermented vegetable matter. Dogs also scavenge dropped over-ripe fruit, berries and seeds, as well as herbivorous dung from the 'jungle floor'.

Cats in the wild eat whole fresh rodents, marsupials, birds, fish, insects, eggs and other animals' leftover prey, and graze on fresh grass and herbs.

What follows is as close to such a diet as we can manage in suburbia, substituting fish oil, vegetables, fruit and herbs to provide the nutrients that would be provided in the wild by rotting seeds from the jungle floor and the semi-fermented gut contents of the wild dog or cat's prey.

Approximately 60–90% by weight of your pet's

total diet should be made up of raw meat and raw bone, and some fish. The remaining 10–40% could be vegetables, fruit, offal, egg, or low-fat dairy products, with a small amount of wholegrain or bran, and generally with added fish oil and herbs to supply a full range of nutrients essential to the animal's health.

60–90% raw meat and raw fat, raw bone, offal, fish

10–40% vegetables, fruit, herbs, fish oil, maybe some wholegrain/bran.

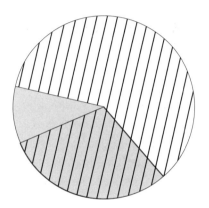

A more detailed breakdown of the above summary is:

- 35% raw muscle meat (including 5–15% raw fat)
- 25% raw bone
- 5–10% raw offal (liver, tripe, kidney, pancreas, heart, tongue), or weekly cod liver oil and wheatgerm oil (1–5 teaspoons), or 50-500 IU vitamin E
- up to 10% fish, egg, low-fat yoghurt/soft cheese — optional
- up to 30% vegetables and fruit
- fish oil or coconut oil (1–6g)

- kelp and/or alfalfa and/or spirulina (½–2 teaspoons powder)
- flax meal and/or bran (½–2 teaspoons), optional
- up to 5% quality cooked grain for special needs pets (eg. lactating pets, thin active animals, puppies, older animals with poor digestion).

Raw meat and raw bone

Raw meat and bone should comprise the greater part of most of meals. Raw meat contains mainly amino acids, which are protein building blocks. It also contains fatty acids, phosphorous and other minerals, and vitamins A, B and E. Bone contains calcium phosphate, collagen and other minerals and nutrients. Bone marrow also contains fatty acids and other useful fat-soluble nutrients.[39]

Even though it may be tempting to feed the bones from roast meat or chops or a cooked chicken, it is really important that you *never* feed cooked bone, as the molecules are set by the cooking process, making it indigestible and dangerous.

In general, it is best to feed different types of white and red meat and offal, as the variety adds nutrients to the pet's diet over the long term. This variety can be spread over a couple of weeks, it doesn't have to be all in one meal. Having a lot of freezer space helps with cost and convenience, but a raw diet still works well for weekly shoppers. The percentage amounts given can be spread over a week or two. So if you run out of offal, kelp, fish or chicken wings, you have a week or two to buy them!

The beauty of natural feeding is that once you understand the principles, a lot of variation is possible. Nature works best with variety, as nature is seasonal and changeable.

Where possible, feed cuts of meat and bone that are not generally eaten by humans. These are cheaper and usually better for dogs and cats as they contain a variety of fat, tendon, cartilage, marrow, muscle and bone nutrients.

Chicken and turkey
Wings, backs and necks for dogs and cats and whole frames (what remains after the breast, wings and legs have been removed) for dogs are easy and cheap to buy from the supermarket. The breast (if it is on the bone), legs and drumsticks are also fine, but more expensive.

Chicken necks are good for cats, puppies and small breed dogs, or mixed with other foods for larger dogs who chew well, otherwise they are likely to be swallowed without chewing.

It is better for bones to be chewed before swallowing, as this is the best way to keep your pet's teeth clean. The chewing also opens up the surface area for better nutrient digestion.

Chickens and turkeys fed on feed or grain that is not organically grown will likely contain some pesticide residue.[40] Free-range poultry is always healthier, for you and your pets. Free-range neck or wing packs are not so expensive, but don't feel too worried if you can't buy it; it is an optional extra. Many of my clients' pets prefer free-range chicken; some do not differentiate and do very well on ordinary supermarket chicken.

Lamb

Lamb is a relatively clean and cheap meat, so raw lamb necks, lamb shanks or other suitable cuts that your pet will chew are good.

Mutton is good too, though adult sheep have been dipped, drenched and dosed more often than lambs, so the meat is not quite as clean.[41] (This also applies to beef.) Being quite a fatty meat, mutton is better for lean, active dogs rather than plumper, more sedentary ones. Cats can tolerate, and need, a lot more fat than dogs.

Rib bones do not suit all pets as they can stick across the roof of the mouth between the top teeth. This is not dangerous but can be a nuisance to remove.

Buying a quarter of mutton can be a very inexpensive way to provide meat, fat and bone for your pets.

Kangaroo

Kangaroo is a very lean meat and is available in supermarkets as chunks of meat for pets, but you need to add an equivalent amount of raw bone to provide the calcium/phosphorous balance. Chicken frames and necks are nearly all bone, so these would be good to combine with roo meat.

Even better is to buy roo on the bone. Roo tails and other cuts can be economical, and can be bought from pet shops and some butchers.

Roo is great for pets needing to lose weight, but not so good for young puppies, nursing mums or thin animals. A more fatty meat such as mutton or lamb would be a better choice for these higher energy need pets.

When buying roo meat, make sure it is a dull maroon colour, not a nice red, as the red colour means preservative has been used. Preservative is not necessary and should be avoided, as it can cause nasty reactions in some animals.

Beef

The cheaper cuts of beef, such as ox tail, are better; the larger leg and spinal bones are too solid for most dogs and cats. A cow is a larger animal than a dog or a cat would naturally predate in the wild, and is not always the best choice of bone.

The long leg beef marrow bones can be too hardwearing on dogs' teeth, and in time may wear the teeth down, causing cracks or exposing the pulp cavity, necessitating specialist dental work.

As well as possible dental damage, these very large hard bones may be too solid to digest fully and can cause problems such as constipation. This can be true of the large bones of any large animal.

Beef is a common cause of itchy allergic skin in dogs and cats. This may be due to the high pesticide residue — cows are drenched and dipped with parasiticide chemicals and usually fed grain sprayed in vermin-deterring chemicals or it may be a straight protein allergy, possibly because the meat is from an animal which is not natural prey.

Some pets are, however, fine with beef, and variety is good, so I suggest adding a small amount of the smaller cuts to the diet.

Less common meats
If your pet has itchy skin, stop feeding beef to see if the problem abates. Substitute a type of meat it has not been fed before — goat, pork, venison, donkey, horse and game are all good options for allergic pets if you can buy them easily and economically. Your pet is less likely to have developed an allergy to these uncommon proteins.

Rats, mice, rabbits, chickens and turkeys that die from known non-infectious causes or are caught without poison are natural and healthy foods. These are the real whole-carcass meals we are trying to copy, so do not waste them (though first remove any large feathers from fowls).

CAUTION: Never feed large herbivore meat (beef, mutton, venison, etc) from an unlicensed shooter or straight from a friend's farm, as the offal may contain hydatid cysts, which are harmful to humans. Meat bought at a supermarket or butcher has been abattoir checked so is safe. If you buy from a pet shop, ask how the meat is procured.

Organic or biodynamically grown meat is, of course, healthier for dogs as it is for us,[42] but we need to stay within our budgets: whatever raw meat and bone you can afford is always healthier than processed food.

Ground bone for puppies and kittens and other special cases

Very young puppies and kittens cannot chew raw bone. They would initially get calcium from their mother's milk and puppies in the wild would eat chewed, semi-digested, regurgitated raw meat and bone from other adults of the pack.[43]

Puppies and kittens need a very high bone component in their diet to keep up with calcium needs of rapid growth, and may not be competent at chewing bone to eat the volume required. Pregnant and lactating bitches of large breeds generally cannot eat enough to cover their calcium needs, whether they are on a natural or processed diet.

Some adult dogs and cats cannot eat any cuts of raw bone. This may be due to the shape of the head of some small breeds, or having an under or overshot jaw or some other conformational abnormality. Or it may be due to accident or injury to head or jaw, or to having lost too many teeth. These individuals may need their raw bone ground or minced with the raw meat to provide the necessary calcium to balance the phosphorous of the meat. Ground bone can be added to the diet in the same proportions as raw bone. You will need a sturdy mincer or food processor to grind bone.

Some butchers, pet shops and chicken outlets sell ground chicken frame mince for pets, which is good inexpensive food for kittens, puppies and dogs who can't chew whole bone. Some butchers will give you the fresh raw bone 'saw dust' from their chopping block, which is a vastly superior product to the processed by-products in many pet foods.

Dr Ian Billinghurst markets an excellent frozen product for cats and dogs needing a ground-bone based diet (it can also be added to whole raw bones for normal adult dogs).[44]

A ground meat and bone mix must never be cooked — all bone should always be fed raw.

Artificial calcium supplements
It is not a good idea to substitute calcium powder or processed bone meal (found in most commercial pet foods) for raw ground bone. Use only fresh raw bone products. Your pet's body cannot easily regulate how much calcium is absorbed from artificial calcium supplements, and it may end up with a deficiency or excess of calcium. This is why it is difficult to get exactly the right calcium compounds from processed commercial food.[45] Bitches and queens prone to milk fever do best on natural calcium-containing foods such as raw bone or, if really necessary, liquid calcium supplements, rather than powdered calcium or processed food containing poor quality bone meal.

The best calcium-supplying foods for cats and dogs are raw bone or raw ground bone, egg shell, low fat yoghurt and low fat cheese. Lots of raw bone in the diet will only improve calcium metabolism, not hinder it.

There is no danger that dogs and cats will accumulate too much calcium from raw bone, so puppies and kittens can and should be fed a very high component of raw meat and bone — approximately 70–90% of the total diet.

All breeding cats and dogs and their young, especially the large breeds of dog such as the Great Dane, Irish Wolfhound, Newfoundland, German Shepherd and Labrador, can benefit from a combination of homeopathic Calcium Phosphate 6X, Calcium Fluorate 6X, Calcium Carbonate 6X and Silicea 6X. This is safe and a few drops can be easily dosed daily in the water bowl of puppies, kittens and pregnant and lactating bitches and queens to help optimise natural calcium metabolism.

Raw fat

Raw fat is essentially covered in the sections on meat and bone because fat comprises up to 15% of raw meat and bone marrow. However it deserves special consideration because we need to view fat very differently from the way we do in a human diet.

Veterinarians may have been taught that too much animal fat is bad for dogs and can cause acute pancreatitis and liver disease. Many vets have treated very sick dogs, some of them even dying from acute pancreatitis after being fed the cooked fat that was cut from a roast dinner or from barbecued steaks.

While too much *cooked* fat can cause problems, *raw* fat and liquid nutritional oils are safe.

This is another good reason not to routinely feed dogs large amounts of cooked meat, as the fat component will obviously be cooked too. (Cooked fat has been shown to be bad for people also, and we are recommended to consume cold pressed oils or fish to get our fatty acid requirements.)

Due to the low pH of the dog and the cat stomach, these animals can easily digest raw fat as about 5–15% of the total diet. This raw fat is a source of nutrient, and should be the primary source of energy, as dogs and cats should not rely on carbohydrates for their energy requirements.[46]

> **Raw fat is an important dietary component, both for nutrition and as the main energy source.**

As an energy source, fat is more useful for thin or energetic cats and dogs than for pets with a tendency to overweight, as excess fat will convert to body fat.

Raw offal or organ meats

In the wild, dogs and cats eat offal along with the rest of the carcass. Offal constitutes about 5–15% of the total carcass,[47] and includes liver, kidneys, heart, tongue, reproductive organs, lungs, brains, pancreas, stomach (tripe) and intestines. These organs all contain nutrients that may not be present in muscle meat, so a variety improves the nutrient base of the diet.

Liver

Liver is probably the most useful offal component of a natural diet. It is high in vitamin A as well as some minor essential fatty acids, and contains some of the nutrients of metabolism such as inositol, methionine and choline. Feeding liver to pets with liver disease is a good idea, especially if they like to eat liver.

However because vitamin A is one of the few vitamins that can be given in excess, it is best not to exceed 5% of the total diet over a long period of time.

If your pet eats a lot of pumpkin, sweet potato, carrots or other betacarotene or vitamin A containing vegetables, then the need for liver in the diet diminishes. Some cats and dogs refuse liver, but eat plenty of yellow vegies, so maybe they are just saying, 'I have enough vitamin A in my diet already, thanks.'

Another way to add liver to the diet is with the air-dried liver treats commonly available.[48] These contain no carbohydrates or artificial additives and are excellent training treats too.

It is easy to make your own liver treats by slicing liver, placing it flat on baking trays in a very low oven, or in a dehydrating unit. Low heat and slow cooking will destroy only a minimal proportion of nutrients.

Since the liver is the organ whose job it is to accumulate toxic chemicals, biodynamic or organic would be best.[49] Otherwise, chicken or turkey giblets or lamb liver are likely to have less pesticide residue than beef or mutton liver.

If you want to avoid handling liver, you can simply add cod liver oil to your pet's food once or twice weekly. Cod liver oil is mainly vitamins A and D, and about 25% omega-3 fatty acids. However I do not generally recommend cod liver oil as a primary omega-3 supplement.

It may be difficult to reach the higher than average amounts required for some animals prone to skin disease without, over a long period of time, overdosing vitamin A, which can interfere with calcium metabolism. Generally, though, there is less chance of overdosing than underdosing vitamin A (see page 106).

Kidneys
The vitamin A content in kidneys is not as high as in liver, so it is safer to feed in larger amounts, up to 10% of the total diet. Animals with kidney disease will often have a good appetite for it, which makes sense as they are consuming the nutrients needed for kidney function. Raw chicken backs often have the kidneys attached; if so, no further kidney will need to be added to the diet.

Pancreas and tripe

Pancreas and tripe contain digestive enzymes, which would contribute greatly to the digestive process of a wild cat or dog eating a whole carcass. Add at least once or twice weekly, but preferably daily. Unfortunately they are not that easy to find but try asking your pet food supplier or your butcher.

I have known dogs with severe exocrine pancreas insufficiency, whose diet has been well managed without the use of enzyme supplements. A third or half of a sheep or beef pancreas fed daily with the meal allows full digestion without further supplements.

When 'green' tripe and pancreas are present in a meal, the dog will digest all nutrients far more efficiently — they effectively improve the 'fuel economy' of the dog — so you can actually get away with feeding less food.

Tripe should be unbleached. The clean white tripe displayed in the supermarket fridge has no active enzymes left in it. Unbleached or 'green' tripe is rather smelly to deal with, but can be frozen and thawed for easier handling.

Digestive enzyme supplements

Digestive enzymes in tablet or powder form could

arguably be used instead of pancreas or tripe. They can be therapeutic given short term for some animals with certain health problems, but if given to a normal healthy animal long term, they may eventually suppress normal enzyme production, although this is not proven.

Ideally it is better therefore to use pancreas and tripe in the normal healthy pet's diet. It is always better to use the real food than a manufactured supplement. Most pets seem to do well without pancreas, tripe or digestive enzymes. It is an option to add digestive enzymes intermittently, instead of regularly feeding tripe or pancreas.

Other offal meats
Heart and tongue contain useful nutrients so are good to add if available and economical. Remember to balance with bone to avoid calcium deficiency.

Lung, throat and oesophagus have less nutritional value than the other offal meats. Trachea contains cartilage rings which are a good bone substitute.

Brain and testes are good foods and are rich in fatty acid, but usually not easily available or affordable.

Yoghurt, eggs, cheese
Eggs and dairy can be added as about 5% of the total diet, replacing any of the other components.

Many dogs and cats are lactose intolerant, and will usually handle goat or sheep or soy milk better than cow's milk, although other than for puppies and kittens, milk is not a natural food, so I generally do not recommend it routinely for adult pets.

Low fat yoghurt and low fat soft cheese are excellent foods in moderation. They are also natural foods of dogs and cats in the wild, as fermented milk would be present in the gut of young prey.

Low fat yoghurt and cheese can be given in greater amounts for puppies and pregnant or lactating bitches and queens, as a way of boosting calcium when they cannot consume enough raw bone.

Dogs in the wild would steal eggs from low nests or scavenge eggs dropped on the ground. Egg yolks are highly nutritious, and have been found to reduce the spread of metastatic cancer.[50] Their high choline level also helps the digestion of fatty acids and fat-soluble vitamins.

Egg whites contain a component which destroys vitamin B1. However, this would only become a problem if frequently feeding a quantity of egg whites alone, as egg yolk contains more vitamin B1 than the whites can destroy.

Vegetables and fruit

Dogs and cats in the wild eat fresh intestinal contents from a herbivore carcass and dogs naturally eat rotting fruit and berries and

herbivorous dung from the forest or jungle floor.
If we cannot provide these natural ingredients for
our pet, we need to add about 10–30% vegetable
matter to their diet to provide the necessary trace
elements, vitamins and vegetable fibre which would
be consumed in the wild.

I have some clients who have lifted the lid off
their compost heap and their dog has eagerly
devoured this wonderful feast! This is fine if there
are no fruit stones, cooked bones, cooked fat or
peel from non-organic vegetables in the heap. I am
not suggesting you make a habit of feeding your pet
compost, rather illustrating the type of food which
is natural to a cat's or dog's digestion.

Add up to 30% raw, pulped or cooked vegetables,
fruit and herbs of as great a variety as possible to
the 70% or so of raw meat, bone and offal. In the
case of an overweight pet, you could increase the
vegetables to 50% to lower the protein level.

The greater the variety of vegetables and herbs, the more likely all necessary nutrients will be present. The fibre and moisture of vegetables will counteract the tendency to dry stools from very high bone diets.

We can't replicate exactly the fermentation process in the herbivore stomach and intestines, but pulping, grating or cooking tough or hard vegetables approximately copies the herbivore chewing and grinding process.

Feed pumpkin, sweet potato, carrot, broccoli, celery, cauliflower, brussel sprouts, zucchini, squash, swede, turnip, parsnip, artichoke, fennel, avocado (flesh, but not skin or seed), beans of all types, spinach, rocket, bok choy, lettuce and other salad greens, tomato, capsicum, cucumber, peas, cabbage, mushroom, beetroot, chick peas and the leaves, flowers, seeds and roots of common culinary herbs.

Many minerals and other nutrients are digested most efficiently from vegetables, fruit and herbs in complex combinations. We know from research studies that iron requires vitamins A and C to be absorbed, copper requires cobalt, and selenium needs vitamin E. There are likely to be many more combinations that presently only nature knows about.

For healthy animals it is better to give nutrients
e form of food rather than in a vitamin tablet

or as an artificial additive in commercial foods which may have been heated and pressurised. The nutrients are more likely to be utilised from a food than in an artificial supplement.

Organic or biodynamic vegetables and herbs are more likely to contain a greater array of nutrients than those grown with pesticides and petrochemical fertilisers.

Feed your dog or cat the vegetables and fruit you find easy to prepare, or that are left over, or are being prepared for humans that day, so no extra work is required. Feed the vegetables and fruit your pet likes best! This often relates to the nutrients the animal actually requires.

Not all dogs like fruit, while some prefer fruit to vegetables. Cats are fussier, but may like one or two fruits or vegetables. There is no point forcing an animal to eat something it doesn't like — the food is probably of no particular use anyway.

Check your fruit bowl and pick out the fruit that is slightly over ripe, though not rotten or mouldy. Brownish bananas, soft pears, nectarines, berries, peaches, apricots, bruised apples, and melon just on the turn are all good pet food. Remove stone fruit pips as they can get stuck in the digestive system. Cut the fruit into pieces or add to vegetables for pulping.

Coconut (fresh or desiccated) and coconut milk are also very good foods.

Some dogs and cats cannot digest insoluble fibre such as pea, corn and lentil skins, apple peel and cabbage spine. These may pass out in the faeces undigested, which won't cause the animal a problem, except perhaps flatulence, which might be a problem for you!

There are rare reports of dogs having a sudden severe kidney problem from eating raisins or grapes. This may be due to an unusual individual reaction to the spray used on the fresh fruit, or the preservative used on the dried fruit. Many dogs and cats happily eat home-grown grapes and dried fruit. To be safe, avoid these foods or only feed organic or unsprayed grapes and dried fruit until more is known about this.

'Jungle floor droppings'

To create your own 'jungle floor', keep a lidded container on the kitchen sink or in the fridge, into which you can put suitable foods to use in you pet's meals which you have accumulated during the day.

Make sure no bread, cake, biscuits or other refined or processed carbohydrate, or cooked bone goes in there — I have to check my dog's bin carefully as my husband and teenage son still sometimes throw in bread crusts!

'Jungle floor' droppings could include carrot and tomato tops, peel of organic vegetables, apple cores; uneaten, bruised or over-ripe fruit (without the pip); broken eggs, leftover salad (but not onion); newly expired yoghurt or fruit juice; pulp left over from juicing fruit and vegies; leftover porridge, soups, stews and stir-fries, and any vegetable, fruit, herb, meat, fish and egg scraps from human meal leftovers. Use within two days.

CAUTION: cooked meat scraps kept for too many days can harbour food poisoning organisms such as Listeriosis, which can cause symptoms in cats and dogs. Raw meat is unlikely to do this, as evidenced by dogs burying bones and eating them days or weeks later with no ill effect.[51]

Cooked vegetables and fruit
Cooking vegetables or stewing fruit reduces some nutrient and enzyme content, but allows for easier digestion. This is good for some individuals, especially older animals or those with digestive deficiencies. According to Chinese medicine theory, it is better to cook vegetables in winter for animals who feel the cold.[52]

You could give your pet whatever cooked vegetables, juice or fruit your family is having th day. If using juice pulp, also sometimes feed complete cooked, grated or pulped vegetables too. If you add herbs (see pages 93–96), it is less important to worry about feeding a full range of vegetables.

Some cats and dogs will not eat any fruit or vegetables. Do not worry; just adding a smear of kelp, alfalfa or spirulina powder to their meat, bones and fish will ensure a full array of trace elements and vitamins.

Vegetarianism

Vegetarianism is not possible for cats; they are obligate carnivores, which means they must have meat in their diet. It is a possibility for some dogs, using nuts, seeds, legumes, peas, beans and dairy products, but is not an ideal or natural way for dogs to be fed. This is too complicated an issue for me to deal with in this book. Juliette de Bairacli Levy has written on this subject.[53]

Vegetable cautions

Onion is poisonous

- Onion is poisonous to dogs and cats — it can dehydrate the red blood cells causing rapid anaemia. A small amount of cooked onion can be tolerated, so feeding a sauce or vegetable dish which contains a small amount of cooked onion is all right. Do not feed any raw onion, and remove any onion from salad before feeding.

- Potato is not a useful vegetable in large amounts as it contains fewer nutrients and more carbohydrate than other vegetables.
- Always remove and discard the peel of non-organic potato and other root vegetables due to possible pesticide residue. The peel of organic foods is safe.
- Green potato peel, rhubarb and silver beet can provide too much oxalic acid if given in excess.
- Very large amounts of raw cabbage, broccoli and brussels sprouts can be toxic. In moderate amounts these are highly beneficial foods, as they contain many useful nutrients including the anti cancer compound indole-3-carbinol.[54] It would be difficult to feed too much of these very useful vegetables.
- Some pips and stones from stone fruit, avocado seeds and tropical fruit pips, skins and seed pods can be poisonous, as can flower bulbs, so do not feed any of these.
- Corn kernels are a good food, but do not feed whole corn cobs, as the cob itself is not digestible and can block the intestines.
- Avoid grapes and dried fruit, unless home-grown, organic or unsprayed.

- Avoid xylitol, a natural sweetener.
- Avoid cocoa bean mulch and large amounts of chocolate because of the toxic theobromide content.
- Many ornamental flowers can be toxic to dogs and cats, so only feed well-known and identified fresh herb plants. Even the water from flower vases can be toxic.
- Aubergine (eggplant), zucchini and tomatoes (all *Solanum* sp.) are more likely than other vegetables to cause allergies. Trial one at a time for pets with skin or bowel allergy symptoms. Meanwhile feed spirulina or alfalfa and no vegetables with meat, bone and coconut oil to maintain a balanced diet while trialling which vegetables your pet may be allergic to.
- Macadamia nuts can be poisonous to some dogs and cats.
- Too many avocados can be detrimental to pets with severe liver disease, but a small amount is beneficial to a healthy pet's diet.

One way to pick your pet's dietary components is to match your animal's tendencies or physical problems with the corresponding foods according to traditional Chinese medicine (see also pages 41, 47 and 87).[55]

Otherwise just feed what is readily available and easy for you to prepare!

Cereals

Except for young puppies and kittens, lactating bitches and queens, and old or unwell dogs and cats with impaired ability to digest, most pets are better off without much carbohydrate. For these special need animals, you could feed up to 10% (by wet weight) of the whole diet from the following nutritious sources of carbohydrate (soaked or cooked to facilitate digestion):

- well soaked or cooked oats, quinoa (highly nutritious, and the best for pups), barley, amaranth, millet, dried peas and beans, lentils, chick peas, polenta (whole ground corn)
- cooked sweet potato, swede, turnip, parsnip, potato
- oat and rice bran (containing calcium and other nutrients) or any other bran.

The largely indigestible fibre or bran part of wheat, barley, oats or rice etc., can provide good roughage to help keep the stools a good consistency — it substitutes for the hair, feathers and other roughage that would be found in a natural whole carcass diet.[56]

A teaspoon to a dessertspoon (depending on size of your pet) of oat bran or flax meal (or any ground or rolled uncooked grain) is good extra roughage in a meal if not already provided by vegetables.

The fibre in bran or flax meal can lower blood glucose in diabetic animals. However do not feed grain (whether whole or refined) to a diabetic animal, as the carbohydrate component may elevate blood glucose levels.[57] Remember, grain is a large component of dried pet food, where it is present as leftovers and by-products that are low in nutrients. Fresh whole grains are far more nutrient rich and therefore a far better source of carbohydrate. Grains and brans can be fed raw, cooked or soaked.

Sugar and sugar-containing foods like chocolate, cake and sweet biscuits, provide empty unneeded carbohydrate, so never feed these.

Pasta and white rice are refined carbohydrates with little benefit nutritionally and generally too high in available carbohydrate to be a suitable component in a dog's or cat's diet.

However, well-cooked white rice can coat the gut and is a good temporary treatment for diarrhoea if slippery elm bark is not available.

Wheat products are generally best avoided as wheat allergy is common in many species, although wheatgerm and wheatgerm oil are good vitamin E supplements for dogs and cats that can tolerate wheat.

A strict no carbohydrate diet is recommended for pets with cancer, to help increase aerobic oxidation which reduces tumour growth.[58]

Herbs

Herbs are highly nutritious and an important part of the diet of many species, including cats and dogs. Add handfuls of basil, parsley, thyme, sage, dill, coriander, oregano, fenugreek, marjoram, dandelion leaf and root, rosemary, turmeric, bay leaf, vervain, mint, fennel, hyssop, garam marsala, ginger, cinnamon, cardamom, lemon balm, cumin, peppermint, spearmint, chamomile, lavender, lemon grass to your pet's food.

The flowers of well known culinary herbs are usually safe and beneficial to feed. (But do not feed ornamental flowers or bulbs, as many are toxic.)

Garlic contains selenium in which many animals and humans are deficient and is essential for the immune system to function.[59] Most patients with recurrent infection or cancer are selenium deficient.[60] Feed up to a quarter to a whole clove daily, depending on the size of your pet. Garlic in excess can cause a similar poisoning to onion, but at these doses it is safe and nutritious.

In our multicultural Australia, we now have a much more adventurous attitude to the use of culinary herbs. The same attitude can be applied to our animal feeding, given some basic knowledge of the herbs we are using.

Herbal medicine v. toxic chemicals
I have read only a tiny fraction of the massive amount of research into herbs carried out across many countries over many decades. Meticulous research has isolated compounds with therapeutic uses, such as immune enhancing, blood glucose stabilising, anti-tumour and anti-inflammatory applications.[61] Studies show, for instance, how specific harmful chemicals are excreted from the liver after dosing with certain herbs.[62]

Many herbs can be used to treat conditions for which conventional medicine lacks safe, effective or economical treatments, such as liver and kidney disease, allergy or poor immunity. The German government's Commission E advises GPs to use any herbs shown to keep people healthy and out of hospitals. This is widely practiced with success, and saves the German government a lot of money.

In this country however, most GPs and veterinarians still commonly use only pharmaceutical single compound drugs to treat their patients. Antibiotics, anti-inflammatory drugs and corticosteroids can be useful, even life saving when disease has progressed to an extreme point, but this reliance on strong drugs seems to be increasing to an unnecessarily high level. As well as excessive pharmaceutical use we have environmental pollution and even the overuse of chemicals for cleaning and pest prevention in the home to create a new range of health problems.[63] Hypothyroidism, for instance has been linked to the chlorine in bleach-based cleaning agents competing with iodine uptake in the thyroid gland.[64]

Fortunately, increasing numbers of biodynamic dairy, beef and other farmers try to avoid using antibiotics for mastitis and the many other conditions generally treated with veterinary drugs. These farmers retain their biodynamic classification by using homeopathics and herbs, which do not leave detectable residue. I hope Australian mainstream agriculture will follow this healthy and sustainable trend, which is more advanced in many European countries.

Based on my personal observation, pets already on natural food and having only minimal necessary vaccination and parasite prevention — especially when this extends over several generations — live on a higher plane of health. Herbs and other natural healing modalities can be more readily effective for these animals.

> **It is better to use a ceramic or stainless steel bowl for your pets, not a plastic one, and to wash it with a chemical-free detergent.[65]**

Certain herbs are effective for particular medical conditions:

- liver detoxification — milk thistle,[66] dandelion root, yellow dock, burdock
- heavy metal toxicity — coriander, milk thistle, green tea
- immunity to bacteria and viruses — echinacea, olive leaf, reishi (ganoderma) and shitaki mushrooms
- bladder infection — cranberry, parsley, couch grass, corn silk, dandelion leaves.
- diarrhoea — slippery elm bark
- travel sickness and vomiting — ginger, peppermint
- constipation — psyllium husks
- anxiety — chamomile, lavender, hops, passionflower
- arthritis — turmeric, ginger
- urinary incontinence in spayed females — sage.

   When considering using a large amount of a particular herb on a long-term basis, always check with your practitioner first.

              ore information, refer to the bibliography
              urray, B. Fougere and J. de Bairacli Levy.

Kelp, alfalfa, spirulina and chlorella

These green plants contain high levels of many essential nutrients: vitamins A, most Bs, C, D, E and K; protein, boron, choline, inositol, iodine, chromium, copper, iron, magnesium, manganese, molybdenum, potassium, silicon, sulphur, selenium and many more phytochemicals.

- Kelp (a seaweed) can be bought as a powder.
- Alfalfa (lucerne) is used as the dried plant. Its long roots take up many nutrients from the soil.
- Spirulina and chlorella are small sea algae which are generally used dried.

If you added no vegies to your pet's meal, one or more of these four herbs would provide most, if not all, of the nutrients needed and for this reason they are recommended as supplements to a raw meat and raw bone diet. They also make excellent routine supplements — they are generally cheaper than multivitamin pills and their nutrients are more easily digested. They can be bought from health food shops, chemists, stock feed supplies or via the internet.[67]

A general dose for kelp is one level teaspoonful per 40kg bodyweight to each meal. For alfalfa, two heaped teaspoons for a 40kg dog per meal. For cats and toy dogs, a pinch of either of these is sufficient.

**For the widest nutrient base, mix one part kelp powder with three parts alfalfa powder, then add one and a half heaped te
of this mix per 40kg body weight ₚ**

Being a sea plant, kelp contains a fairly high level of iodine, and can be helpful in the treatment of hypothyroidism (underactive thyroid). Hypothyroidism may present as repeated skin infection, thinning hair, overweight, constipation and low energy.

CAUTION: do not use kelp for pets diagnosed with or suspected of having hyperthyroidism (an overactive thyroid gland).

Spirulina and chlorella are more expensive. Dose proportionately per body weight according to the recommended human dose for your product (an average adult human can be assumed to be 60–80kg).

Spirulina is recommended for pets with cancer as it contains an important anti-cancer pigment phycocyanin.[68]

If your pet is on chemotherapy for cancer, changing to a natural diet, cutting out carbohydrates, and introducing these supplements, and antioxidants, will help, not hinder, the effectiveness of the chemotherapy, a concern often raised by pet owners.[69]

Herbs for dogs and cats who refuse vegetables
For pets who refuse larger portions of vegetables, it is often possible to smear meat and bone with

these herbs. If you feed *no* vegetables, but just the recommended amounts of these herbs, you will probably end up feeding about 90% raw meat, fat, fish, bone and offal. For the few pets that still refuse vegetables after a three or four week conversion period, using these herbs works well to balance their diet.

In this situation, it would be advisable to add some fibre, ideally in the form of flax meal. Psyllium husks are the best first aid treatment for constipation. They are usually available in the cereal section of a supermarket, or from a chemist or health food shop. Add between a pinch and a teaspoonful to a meal.

Sprouted grains, grasses and seeds

Barley or wheat grass and sprouted beans and seeds can be fed fresh if you sprout them yourself and, with their chlorophyll content, are wonderful nutrition. Beware, though, that sprouts can harbour food poisoning organisms if left until over ripe, or if they are too moist or not washed frequently.

There are also many brands of barley or wheat grass. It is not known if dogs and cats can break down the cell walls to obtain full nutrient components of wheat and barley grass, so pulping or powdering would aid digestion.

Unsalted nuts and pumpkin, sunflower or s~~~ seeds and pine nuts, ideally ground or hamme aid digestion, can be fed to dogs and cats and are very nutritious, but do not feed unknown seeds or macadamia nuts.

Flax meal, flax oil and fish oil

The best form of fibre to add to a pet's diet is flax meal which is ground flax seed, also known as linseed. Flax meal contains oligofructosaccaride, a soluble fibre which acts as a substrate for 'good' bowel bacteria to feed on, thus maintaining these bacteria in the bowel. A food which acts this way is called a prebiotic (see 'Probiotics and Prebiotics' below). Prebiotics enhance the immune system by preventing harmful bacteria an entry point in the gut.

Many naturopaths recommend you grind your own 'LSA' — ground linseed (flax seed), sunflower seed and almond meal. If you keep LSA in the house for human consumption, add one heaped teaspoon per 40kg body weight (a pinch for cats and toy breed dogs) to your pet's food.

Omega-3 and omega-6

Veterinary dermatologists say that some cats and dogs prone to allergies need omega-3 at a rate many times higher than the average. I have often found this to be the case for pets with itchy skin conditions. If in doubt, increase the amount of fish oil in your pet's diet. The worst side effect will be loose stools, so cut back on the oil until stools are firm again.

Feed ground flax for its lignan (fibre) content but use fish oil as the major fatty acid component of a dog's diet.

Dogs and cats are likely to have enough omega-6 from the meat, offal, vegies and herbs in their diet, but they need about six times more omega-3 than omega-6.

The two important omega-3 fatty acids for dogs and cats are docosahexaenoic acid (DHA) and eicosapentaenoic acid (EPA). There is evidence that EPA and DHA can prevent and treat many health conditions, such as skin, eye and joint disease.[70]

However, in order to access the DHA and EPA from flax and sunflower oils, dogs and cats need to carry out two biochemical processes and some cannot do this effectively. For those animals, the fatty acids in flax and sunflower seeds are 'inactive', and their response to flax or sunflower oil for conditions such as skin allergy or rheumatoid arthritis is less predictable than it is in humans. For this reason, it is best to give omega-3 in the form of small cold-water fish, or fish oil, to all pets.

Fish and fish oil
Mackerel, sardine, pilchard, salmon, herring and whitebait are the most easily available small cold-

water fish. Large fish such as tuna and shark are not so high in omega-3, and can concentrate heavy metals as they are top of the food chain.

For dogs who are allergic to all meat I have used fish instead of the raw meat and bone component of the diet. This is a rare thing to have to do, but the dogs did well.

Fresh, frozen or tinned fish making up about 10% of the total diet would give the required omega-3 for most dogs and cats. Additional fish oil capsules or liquid will ensure you have provided enough of this essential nutrient. If your pet's coat is silky smooth and healthy and rarely needs washing, they are getting enough omega-3 in their diet.

Fish oil is not cod liver oil. Cod liver oil contains about 25% omega-3 and 75% vitamin A and D. Fish oil is primarily omega-3 fatty acids.

There are some good combination liquid oil products available for cats and dogs.[71] I usually recommend fish oil as it is the best quality active omega-3 supplement and I can rely on it working better than any combined products for those difficult itchy skin cases. Try your preferred supplements for your pet to know which will be best — it takes about two weeks for the coat to become more shiny and strong when an omega-3 deficiency has been orrected.

The dose of fish oil is from 500mg for cats or a toy breed dog to 6000mg for a large breed dog, or even more if allergic symptoms dictate.

Fish oil capsules are generally 1000mg. More expensive brands will have higher amounts of EPA and DHA, so check this to determine value between brands.

When your pet is allergic to fish
Coconut oil is an excellent substitute for animals allergic to fish. Feed the same number of grams as fish oil. Fresh or desiccated coconut and coconut milk are excellent foods for dogs and cats and can safely be fed regularly.

To make a good fibre and omega-3 supplement, mix desiccated coconut with oat bran and flax meal in equal parts. Store in the fridge and add a pinch to a handful regularly to your pet's food.

Other supplements
There are a few excellent products which combine kelp, flax meal, rice bran, alfalfa, spirulina, chlorella and powdered vegetables such as carrot, apple, berries and other nutrients.[72]

If you use these products, you must still add the fish or fish oil for the necessary omega-3 content in the diet.

Be careful to check that your pet does not have allergies to any ingredients of these combination products Dried beef liver is a common allergen which may be an ingredient. Otherwise, these make excellent supplements.

Yeast is a common inclusion as it contains the B vitamins, but make sure that it is a nutritional yeast not brewer's or baker's yeast (which have a tendency to ferment). Yeast is not needed if kelp and alfalfa are fed, although some animals like the taste, so you may choose to use yeast instead.

Tamari, tahini, miso and lecithin are all useful supplements if you have them to hand and if your pet likes them.

I do not recommend additive mixes which contain added calcium or processed bone meal for reasons discussed on page 75 (although freshly ground raw bone in a raw meat product is good) and I don't routinely use products with added vitamin C[73] (see also page 107).

Prebiotics and probiotics

Probiotics are supplements of the live normal, useful bowel bacteria such as *Bifidus* and *Lactobacillus* species. These can be found in yoghurt in low amounts or in specific supplements in higher amounts.

Probiotics are often used to treat dysbiosis (unbalanced bowel flora) by putting back the beneficial bacteria into the gut.[74] Dysbiosis can cause diarrhoea, fungal infections or even ongoing irritable bowel disease. Causes of dysbiosis include prolonged antibiotic or corticosteroid treatment, stress or poor diet.

Poor digestion and dysbiosis can predispose an animal to allergy (asthma or allergic skin disease) or autoimmunity in later life, reinforcing the importance of feeding a balanced natural diet.[75]

Saccharomyces boulardii is a yeast organism probiotic which is both stable and very quick acting. It can clear up a dose of food poisoning diarrhoea caused by bacteria or protozoa within hours by physically binding with the pathogenic organisms.[76]

Probiotics such as *Saccharomyces* are therefore a good initial treatment for dysbiosis, best followed with 'good bacteria' probiotics such as *Lactobacillus* and *Bifidus* to repopulate the bowel back to normal levels.

It is no use dosing probiotics while the animal is on antibiotics, as antibiotics kill these good bowel bacteria. Start the probiotics as soon as the antibiotics finish and treat for about a month. Follow with flax meal for maintenance. A soluble fibre like flax meal is called a 'prebiotic' in this situation, as the content assists the production of good bowel bacteria without actually adding them, by providing a substrate to feed on. Prebiotics can replace the need for, or continue the good work of, probiotics.

Vitamins and antioxidants
Vitamin A
Vitamin A is an essential antioxidant fat-soluble nutrient present in liver (including fish liver oils, but not fish oil), and to a lesser extent kidney, also in orange vegetables such as carrot, sweet potato, pumpkin, spinach and to a lesser extent in other foods. Daily requirements for vitamin A are 1000 to 10,000 IU daily, depending on body size, but it rarely needs adding in extra amounts if the general diet protocol is followed.

There has been a lot of publicity about excess vitamin A causing calcium imbalance in humans. This can also happen to cats and dogs if liver or supplements are fed daily in doses far greater than the daily requirement, for weeks or months on end. Overdose is also possible if halibut liver oil is fed, which is extremely high in vitamin A.

In general however, vitamin A is more likely to be underdosed than overdosed. Dosing with cod liver oil or feeding liver at about 5% of the total diet presents *no* danger of overdosing either vitamin A or D.

Feed liver (or liver treats) as about 5% of the diet, or orange vegies, or cod liver oil once or twice weekly, to ensure sufficient vitamins A and D.

I might further supplement vitamin A for animals with bone cancer, degenerative myelopathy, auto-immune disease, chronic respiratory tract infection and some types of eye disease. Bilberry is rich in betacarotene, the metabolic precursor of vitamin A, and is in many eye supplements for this reason.

Vitamin C
Add vitamin C to a pet's diet *only* in times of reduced immunity such as infection, allergy, cancer, autoimmunity, accident or emotional stress.[77] At these times, megadose vitamin C to bowel tolerance. This means increasing the dose with each meal until it causes soft stools. Then reduce the dose until stools are the right consistency. That way, you will be giving the highest dose the body requires for immune function.

If the pet is well, don't give vitamin C at all, otherwise the body can get lazy and rely on it, and the body's natural production may drop.

Do NOT routinely add vitamin C to a healthy pet's food.

If using vitamin C megadosed to bowel tolerance, use ascorbic acid, as cats and dogs need more acidity than humans (for whom the alkaline sodium ascorbate is often recommended).

This is especially so if the animal has had urinary tract infections or bladder stones which dissolve in an acidic urine. It would be harmful to dose a urinary alkalinising agent such as sodium ascorbate in this type of case. Calcium ascorbate is of neutral pH so is safer, though not proactively helpful in lowering urinary pH.

Vitamin E

The fat-soluble antioxidant vitamin E is found in raw red meat, liver, seeds, nuts, oily herbs, wheat germ and green leafy vegies. Most natural diets contain sufficient vitamin E, but if your pet requires extra vitamin E for a specific health reason, then adding more will do no harm.

If dosing vitamin E in capsule form, give 50 IU daily for cats and small dogs up to 500 IU for large breed dogs.

Squeeze the contents of a capsule onto food, or put the whole capsule in the food if the pet will eat it. Wheatgerm, wheatgerm oil and tahini (ground sesame seed) are other easy ways of adding vitamin E. It is safe to feed these foods routinely and they contain many excellent nutrients.

Dose wheatgerm oil at about a teaspoon to a dessertspoon daily, depending on body size and need.

I would supplement extra vitamin E for patients with low immunity to bacteria, degenerative myelopathy, autoimmune conditions, cancer, and difficult to correct fatty acid deficiency, as vitamin E helps to metabolise fatty acids.

Other antioxidants
Vitamins A, C, D and E are all antioxidants. Grape seed extract, green tea, maritime pine bark, coenzyme Q10 and other antioxidants are also available in different forms and combinations.

Antioxidants bind with and therefore negate the free radicals which cause aging and degeneration of tissue. They can help in severe or chronic disease, especially in ageing pets. I use coenzyme Q10 for pets with heart disease, chronic gingivitis and cancer.

I also supplement the diet with antioxidants for animals with degenerative myelopathy, arthritis, autoimmune disease, cancer and chronic low immunity to infection.

Antioxidants are always beneficial for any old or chronically ill animals. In general, they have no side effects, apart from depleting your budget.

Some sample menus

The following sample meals provide a starting point
for putting together some well-balanced meals
for your pet. The proportions refer to the weekly
ration, so three meals could lack fish, four may lack
offal, one may lack vegetables — if they generally
add up over a week or so, that is enough. The
quantities given are for one day's worth of food.

A 1.3kg meal for a 40kg dog:
- 900g meat, fat, bone, offal (eg, two chicken
  wings, a lamb kidney and a small lamb neck)
- 100g tinned pilchards
- 300g vegies (eg, cooked pumpkin, broccoli stalk,
  carrot tops)
- a dollop of low fat yoghurt
- 2 teaspoons mixed kelp and alfalfa powder
- 4 x 1g capsules of fish oil

A 1 kg meal for a 25kg dog:
- 800g meat, fat, bone, offal (eg, a chicken frame
  and 3 lamb hearts)
- 200g vegies (eg, pulped sweet potato,
  cauliflower, apple)
- 1 handful fresh parsley and basil
- 1 teaspoon kelp
- 2 x 1g fish oil capsules
- 1 dessertspoon flax meal

A 250g meal for a 5kg dog or two 125g meals for a 5kg cat:
- 150g meat, fat, bone (eg, two chicken necks or one chicken wing)
- 50g vegies (eg, mixed juice pulp, banana, ginger peelings)
- 40g of raw white bait
- 1 egg
- 1g capsule of fish oil
- a pinch of kelp
- 1 teaspoon cod liver oil

These meals would still be balanced without the tinned pilchards, raw white bait, egg or yoghurt. But if your pet likes these components, and they are available and convenient, they add extra variety and nutrient.

If cats and small dogs don't readily accept fish oil, kelp and cod liver oil, there is no need to force them on a daily basis. At least once a week is good enough.

The lamb kidney and cod liver oil are good additions once or twice a week, but are not needed every day. You could feed dried liver treats instead.

If no vegies were available, these meals would still be balanced without them, but the vegies provide more fibre and nutrient. Try to include vegetables, fish and yoghurt on some days, but it doesn't have to be every day.

Don't panic!

Very likely you are now feeding a more balanced and complete diet of raw, natural food than you were before embarking upon this adventure, so do not panic about exact percentages!

- Don't be afraid to vary the amounts and components. As long as you stay within the approximate percentages you will not go wrong.
- When you go on holiday and someone else is feeding your pet, do not worry if the diet is not as varied as it would be if you were doing the feeding.
- If you run out of an ingredient, that's all right, you have a week or two to stock up again.

For more sample meals, Mogens Eliasen's *Raw Food for Dogs* offers many variations and menus, as does Erica Williams' natural diet recipe book, *FeedWell* (see the bibliography).

4
principles of feeding cats

Principles of Feeding Cats

Cats are obligate carnivores, which means they *cannot* be vegetarians (unlike dogs for whom vegetarianism is difficult but not impossible). Like dogs they have an acidic stomach, but in general they are more carnivorous than dogs, most cats requiring about 85% raw meat, fat, bone, offal and only 15% vegetables, herbs and roughage. Unlike dogs, they appear to need more frequent feeding: the cat's stomach is small, and it does not expand in the way the dog's does.

Cats in the wild

Cats in the wild would naturally prey on rabbits, mice, rats, other small rodents, eggs, marsupials, birds, insects and lizards. They may also graze on fresh herbs and grasses.

Cats in the wild may occasionally go without food for a few days and this can assist with ridding the body of wastes and chemicals, so can be a beneficial process.

Domestic cats on a natural diet can also safely fast for a day or so. But the liver metabolism of cats fed predominantly commercial dried food is compromised, and cats can suffer hepatic lipidosis if they miss two or more meals.

Raw food and Pottenger's cats

An interesting piece of research which shows the dependence of cats on a mainly raw meat diet was carried out in the 1930s in the United States by top medical researchers under the best experimental conditions of the time.[78] Led by Dr Francis Pottenger Jr MD, this ten-year controlled crossover trial involved about 900 cats, and its major findings occurred partly by accident — as have so many other good scientific discoveries!

In this case, one laboratory of cats was fed their food cooked and another laboratory of cats was fed the same food raw — purely because one of the lab assistants decided to cook the rations and the other didn't!

The cats fed the cooked food had a significantly greater incidence of allergies, skin problems, parasites, skeletal disease, behaviour problems and diseases involving the thyroid, heart, kidney, liver, testes, ovaries and bladder. After three generations, their reproductive health had deteriorated to the point where they were infertile.

However, when the last generation of cooked food cats were fed raw food, they gradually regained their health and fertility, though it took four generations to return to the excellent health of the raw food fed group.

It is likely that the cats fed cooked food lacked certain essential amino acids, primarily taurine, arginine, methionine and cysteine, which are only found naturally in raw meat.[79] These amino acids are now added to most tinned and dried commercial cat foods. This is obviously a good move, but it does not address the high carbohydrate content of dried commercial foods, or the provision of other enzymes and amino acids found only in raw meat.

It is even more necessary for cats than for dogs to have a regular supply of protein as a large percentage of their diet.

On a low protein diet (less than about 80%), cats will break down essential amino acids as a fuel source,[80] to the detriment of other essential processes for health, including the immune system, liver and reproductive metabolism.

Feeding a high percentage of raw meat in a cat's diet may avoid long term degenerative diseases such as idiopathic hepatic lipidosis, diabetes mellitus, kidney disease and inflammatory bowel disease — all caused by lack of plentiful dietary essential amino acid (protein).[81]

It is therefore just as important with cats as with dogs to avoid carbohydrate, or to keep it at a level well below that of the meat and fat percentage.

Digestible carbohydrates should be no more than 3–5% of the total diet for a normal adult non-breeding cat. Raw fat, not carbohydrate, is the correct energy fuel for cats.[82]

About 10% or more of a cat's diet can be fat and fatty meat with benefit. Fish oil can substitute some of this meat fat, but not all.

The problem with dried commercial cat food

Feline specialist veterinarians and scientists increasingly agree that adult cats should not be fed dried commercial cat food due to the processed grain or carbohydrate content. Several veterinary journal articles published over the last few years support feeding cats no dried cat food at all.[83] One suggests that cats fed raw meat may live about fourteen years, compared to about twelve years for cats fed dried food. Some suggest that dental problems occur less often in cats fed a raw diet compared to those fed dried food.[84]

Other diseases suspected to be more common in dried food fed cats are kidney failure, obesity (and therefore arthritis), diabetes, bladder stones, liver disease and irritable bowel disease.[85]

Animals have often been used as research subjects for common human conditions such as diabetes mellitus, and we have good evidence that commercial dried cat food can increase the likelihood of diabetes mellitus in cats, especially if it is left out for the cat to help itself, and most especially if the cat is already overweight.[86]

It is best to feed cats who have recovered from diabetes or hepatic lipidosis no cereal-based dried food at all.[87]

Even the most prestigious dried cat foods can be 25% carbohydrate, which is way above the optimum 3–5%. The carbohydrate percentage may not be stated on the packet, but you can calculate it by adding up the protein, fibre, moisture, fat and other ingredients and deducting that sum from 100%.

The law does not require that pet foods contain a certain quality of protein or cereal in the way that it does for foods for human consumption. Often, the protein content is primarily comprised of 'meat meal' or 'meat by-product'. These are not obliged to be anything more nutritious than claws, beaks, feathers etc. Cereal 'by-products' can literally be sweepings from the grain factory floor. This could have been the cause of melamine waste contamination in premium dried pet food in the United States recently, which poisoned several pet animals.

In general, canned foods have lower levels of digestible carbohydrate than dried commercial foods, so are preferable. However the food is still cooked, so does not contain as many amino acids or enzymes as raw fresh meat or even partly cooked fresh meat.

Note that some of the less well-known brands spend more money on product quality than advertising, so it is worth investigating different products.

Liver metabolism

As with dogs, we are concerned with the cat's liver: it is a major digestive organ and very important to long-term health. Liver dysfunction can lead to skin disease, allergy, poor immunity, autoimmunity, degenerative diseases and cancer.[88]

Feeding a cat a diet with higher than about 3–5% carbohydrates can be detrimental to liver metabolism. When excess carbohydrate is used as fuel, the liver does not undergo full glycogen metabolism,[89] which means toxins can remain stored in the liver and fat for years, leading to many possible health problems.[90]

Feeding a cat one or two very low (or no) carbohydrate meals a day will allow for more effective liver metabolism and detoxification, and therefore a healthier cat.

Some commercial cat foods are now being made from air-dried muscle meat, offal, herbs, fish, and fish oil — with little or no grain at all. These products combine well with fresh raw meat and bone by supplying all the other components needed in a cat's diet.[91]

An air-dried product has identifiable ingredients and is manufactured under much lower temperatures and is less dehydrated than many grain-based extruded dried foods. It is also less likely to concentrate the urine and exacerbate the tendency towards forming bladder stones in some cats.

When and how much to feed

Feed cats once or twice daily (most prefer twice). Kittens need more frequent feeding (see page 127).

Do not leave food out if is not eaten straight away.

An adult cat weighing 5kg would eat 3–5% of its body weight or about 200–250g of food per day, divided into two meals each of 100–125g.

5
the changeover process for cats

The Changeover Process for Cats

Most cats are capable of being converted to a totally natural diet.

For some older cats, and some re-homed cats, it may be difficult to change what they eat, as keeping to what they know may help them feel secure. In this case, a more gradual change to the new diet may help.

If cats have been fed high carbohydrate dried food they may be addicted to the blood glucose 'high' that gives. But after a few hours, the cat is hungry again and asking for more food. These cats never feel satisfied with their diet, and not surprisingly. Fortunately, it does not take long to break the addiction.

So many clients report that once they have pushed through a two or three week changeover period, their cat is so much happier and more satisfied with its new diet. It no longer hangs around the kitchen yowling for food, as it now feels satisfied that

the food being given is what it really needs —
which it is.

**The first step to converting your cat to
a natural diet is to leave no food out
between meals. For the first time in its life,
the cat will be genuinely hungry and will
more likely accept the new food.**

Feed two meals daily to begin with; one may be
enough later on, but most cats prefer two.

Start by gradually adding small pieces of raw
chicken neck to the cat's favourite tinned or dried
food. Then add tinned or fresh fish, prawns, cheese,
yeast powder or whatever your cat likes to get them
used to crunching the raw meat and bone pieces.

If your cat likes tinned fish, try substituting raw
whole or tinned small fish (including the bone) for
some meat and bone.

**It is very easy to succeed with a natural
diet if you start at the kitten stage.**

Kittens

It is generally easy to get kittens onto a natural diet.
At weaning time, start them on some milk substitute
from a veterinary clinic, along with the adult natural
diet. Good kitten foods are yoghurt and soft cheese,
ground raw meat and ground raw bone.[92]

As soon as they can manage it, feed kittens plenty of whole raw bone to optimise chewing skills. The pointy bit at the end of a chicken wing is good to start on as soon as the kitten arrives at your house.

It is so good to see a kitten growling and chewing a lump of raw meat and bone while holding it down with its paw. This activity balances serotonin and endorphins in the brain, aiding digestive enzyme release and creating a happy, relaxed and healthy cat.

Raw fat is a kitten's best fuel source, and kittens grow fast, so plenty of raw fat on the meat is good and necessary.

If the kitten has been started on dried food, slowly wean them off over a week or two. Any sudden changes in diet can cause diarrhoea. If this happens, add a pinch of slippery elm bark powder to each meal until the diarrhoea has cleared up. Slippery elm bark powder is a good and harmless diarrhoea prevention and can be given routinely over the settling in period for kittens.

When and how much to feed kittens
Feed newly weaned kittens about a heaped teaspoonful of food four times daily. Thereafter:

- four times daily from weaning to 12 weeks old
- three times daily from 12 to 16 weeks

- two or three times daily from four to six
months
- once or twice daily from six months.

Increase the amount as the kitten grows to approximately 5–10% of its body weight daily, divided into the requisite number of meals. Kittens growing fast will need nearer to 10%.

Sample kitten meals

- ground raw chicken meat and bone mince with a pinch of kelp
- ground raw lamb meat and bone with a pinch of complete supplement[93]
- fresh chopped raw whitebait
- tinned sardines or pilchards
- raw chopped chicken wing ends with a few drops of cod liver oil
- raw egg yolk or scrambled egg with a few drops of fish oil
- oat bran porridge (made with kitten milk substitute from vet)
- roast pumpkin, cut up into small pieces
- sweet potato and carrot mashed with cheese and a pinch of kelp powder
- chopped lamb kidney and a pinch of fresh chopped parsley
- raw chicken necks hammered and chopped into pieces.

6
components of a natural diet for cats

ponents for a

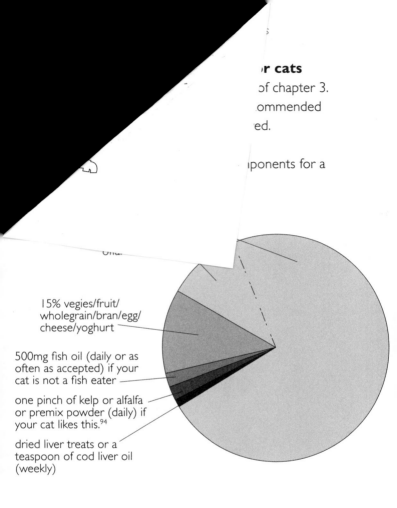

15% vegies/fruit/
wholegrain/bran/egg/
cheese/yoghurt

500mg fish oil (daily or as
often as accepted) if your
cat is not a fish eater

one pinch of kelp or alfalfa
or premix powder (daily) if
your cat likes this.[94]

dried liver treats or a
teaspoon of cod liver oil
(weekly)

It is important that as you feed your
pet this fresh and healthy food you are
confident and proud that you have chosen
for them a diet that Mother Nature would
have intended them to eat!

Raw meat and bone

Raw meat is essential as a large proportion of the cat's diet.[95]

Cats would primarily eat a white meat diet, as natural prey would include mice, rats, rabbits, other small rodents, marsupials, birds, insects and lizards.

Wild cats might sometimes score leftovers from a larger animal's prey, so some red meat is a good inclusion, and red meat contains some nutrients that white meat lacks.

Feed any cuts of raw meat and bone your cat likes and can manage to chew up. Favourites are raw chicken necks, wings and drumsticks, and raw lamb cutlets, necks and shanks.

Some cats like cooked meat. Cooking does reduce the amount of nutrient in meat, so if you cannot get your cat to eat raw meat only, cook the chicken neck or wing only lightly to ensure the bone is still raw, or feed raw meat at some meals and cooked at others. Cats who feel the cold may prefer some cooked lean meat and vegetables/grains, especially in winter.[96]

Offal or organ meat includes liver, kidney, heart, tongue, pancreas, brain, lungs, tripe and would naturally be eaten as about 5% of a whole carcass diet. It provides vitamins A, D and E and fatty acids, choline and other nutrients so is needed to balance a cat's diet.

Liver is very rich in vitamin A. About 5% of the diet as liver would provide enough of this important vitamin. Too much liver can cause an overdose of vitamin A, which might interfere with calcium metabolism, however under-dosing is more common. Kidney and other offal can be given in greater amounts (up to 15%), as they are not so rich in vitamin A.

It is easy to buy chicken giblets (livers), lamb liver, kidney and heart. There are also some good air-dried liver treats available you can use instead of fresh offal.[97]

Pancreas and unwashed tripe are wonderful digestive enzyme supplements but can be hard to find. I have found one air-dried food which has no digestible carbohydrate and contains tripe.[98]

Raw bone keeps a cat's teeth clean and healthy all its life. Cats generally need to chew bones at least five days a week to get enough calcium and to keep their teeth clean. The calcium in bone balances the phosphorous present in large amounts in meat to achieve ideal skeletal health.

Never feed a cat cooked bone, as the molecules are set and made indigestible by the cooking process and can be dangerous.

Raw bone of the appropriate size (eg, a chicken neck or a chopped up chicken neck or wing) is easily digested by a cat's acidic stomach.

A raw chicken neck as the first meal for the day is an economical way to achieve dietary calcium balance and to keep the teeth clean for life.

For the second meal of the day, you can feed raw meat or fish, as well as the vegetable, fruit and dairy components, and supplements, herbs and oils.

Chewing on raw bone is the best way to clean the teeth and to develop healthy jaw and neck muscles in kittens.

Good sized bone, offal and meat cuts for cats

- chicken necks, whole or cut up small to mix through food your cat is used to (while changing to a natural diet)
- turkey necks, hammered or cut into a few pieces
- chicken and turkey wings, hammered and cut up
- small lamb necks cut into parts or hammered
- large diced pieces of red meat
- any other meat or bone you can buy easily which your cat likes and can safely chew several times before swallowing — eg, rabbit, game, venison, goat, pork
- chicken giblets or diced lamb kidne heart.

Fish

Fish is an excellent food for cats, and can substitute for some, but generally not all, of the 85% meat, bone and offal. I have had many clients who live in Fremantle where fish are plentiful and economical, and many

have used whole raw fish as a major part of their cat's diet to good effect.

> **Fish can be a staple food for cats, but the cat must still have some raw meat in its diet.**

Fish washed up on the riverbank would provide wild cats with this food. I have even heard of cats catching fish with their paws.

The best fish for cats are raw whitebait (often sold in frozen blocks for fishermen), pilchard, mackerel, the famous Freo sardine, and even prawns and other seafood. Dried raw bait is a good cat food.

Herring should not be fed continually or as a main protein source, as herring can contain thiaminase which destroys vitamin B1. I have treated one case of thiamine deficiency caused in this way. It was a fisherman's cat, fed only on herring for weeks on end on a fishing trip. When it was brought to me the cat was blind and had been unable to balance at all for several days, but one intravenous injection of thiamine (vitamin B1) reversed the symptoms in hours.

The omega-3 fatty acid in the fish body and liver, and vitamins A and D in the fish liver, are all essential nutrients for a cat, so whole raw fish does seem an appropriate staple food. Omega-3 fatty acids are especially present in the body tissue of the small blue skinned fish varieties named above.

Tinned small fish in oil or spring water or tomato sauce is a good food for cats, if most of the rest of their protein and bone is raw.

Larger fish such as shark, snapper and tuna need the large bones removing before feeding to cats, and extra fish oil needs to be supplemented, as these fish store omega-3 in their liver, not their body tissue. There is less likelihood of heavy metal traces in smaller fish such as pilchard, mackerel and sardine, so ideally these are preferable to tuna.

If you or your cat do not like dealing with raw offal, then a teaspoon of cod liver oil once or twice weekly will supply the cat with vitamin A.

sy way to supply plenty of fatty acids to a cat
x fish oil (omega-3 fatty acids), cod liver oil
(vitamin A) and wheatgerm oil (vitamin E) in equal
quantities and put half a teaspoon on some of the
cat's meals.

Vegetables, fruit, grain, herbs, eggs, yoghurt, cheese

Feeding vegetables, fruit, herbs, eggs and dairy
products completes the cat's diet, providing
nutrients which would naturally be eaten as part of
the intestinal contents of their prey. Together they
should make up about 15% of the cat's total diet.

Vegetables, fruit and grain husks supply the
necessary fibre found in a whole carcass diet to
help soften the stool consistency. A pinch of psyllium
husks (available in supermarkets in the cereal
section) is an easy way to add fibre to prevent
constipation if your cat is not really a vegetable eater.

Herbs are also grazed fresh by wild and
domesticated cats. Catnip (which can send
some cats into a purring, rolling frenzy), cat
grass and other herbs are thought to be
attractive to cats because of their nutrients.

Cats may steal eggs from birds' nests or they may
find them on the ground, rejected from nests, so
these are natural foods for them.

Oats or oat bran, quinoa, amaranth, millet, barley and other whole (unprocessed) grains can be useful in small amounts: cooked or soaked as porridge or a pinch added raw to meat. Do not exceed about 5% of the total diet, as excess carbohydrate does not allow for full liver metabolism to occur.[99]

Yoghurt and soft cheese are as close as we can get to the digested milk in the gut of young prey. The lactose in milk which may cause diarrhoea has mostly been fermented out of yoghurt and soft cheese, so most cats can eat these.

Unlike dogs and humans, cats can generally handle full fat dairy products, however raw fat on meat is the best fat for them in large amounts.

Which vegetables, fruit and herbs you feed your cat will depend a lot on what your cat will eat. I have heard many stories from clients about the particular things their cat loves or hates. One client's cat likes a dressed side salad put next to the meat bowl! Here are some other likes:

- rock melon
- mashed pumpkin, sweet potato or other vegies, especially with cheese or sour cream mixed into it
- cheese grated onto the meal
- fruit and yoghurt
- raw, scrambled or poached egg

es or tinned fish in tomato sauce
    vegetables
        ned vegetables mixed with meat or fish
- canned, creamed or whole corn (but not the cob).
- Generally, a cat will let you know which
  nutrients it requires by favouring some foods
  over others after the changeover period to the
  natural diet.

Nutrient supplements

Kelp and spirulina are the best nutrient supplements
for cats, as they contain a broad array of essential
vitamins and trace elements generally not found
in meat, bone and offal. Adding a pinch of kelp or
spirulina can provide a quick and easy balanced
natural diet for a cat.

Ready made supplement mixes containing flax
meal, kelp, rice bran, alfalfa, broccoli or other
vegetable powders,[100] are even better for fussy
cats, as it is easy to wipe half a teaspoonful of the
powder onto a chicken neck or chunk of meat or
some tinned or raw fish.

Flax meal provides good roughage for cats
who do not eat vegetables, and contains
oligofructosaccharides which good bowel
bacteria thrive on, thus strengthening the cat's
immune system.

Avoid premixed supplements which contain
vitamin C, processed bone meal or calcium powder

as these are best not fed routinely. Calcium is better balanced by feeding raw fresh bone.

Feeding extra vitamin C to a well cat can reduce the cat's natural production of vitamin C, and processed bone meal or calcium powder can easily cause an excess or deficiency of calcium.

Fish oil is essential unless about 10–30% of the cat's diet is small blue skinned fish. Even if a cat eats plenty of fish, it does no harm to give extra fish oil. It seems that some cats cannot synthesise the essential omega-3s EPA and DHA from flax oil.

I suggest adding 500mg fish oil daily to any cat's meal, regardless of the other nutrients present. You can hide a capsule whole in the food, or squeeze the contents of the capsule onto one meal a day, or feed a liquid form of fish oil.

If your cat rejects this, start with a smaller amount and increase it over time until you find the amount your cat is telling you it needs. It may get all its omega-3 requirements from eating fish.

For cats allergic to fish, use coconut oil or coconut milk — both are excellent sources of omega-3 fatty acid.

e sample menus for cats

An adult cat eats about 3–5% of its body weight daily. The following sample meals provide a starting point for putting together some well-balanced meals for your cat. Two meals are given for each body size.

Note: the meals for a 6kg cat assume an overweight animal, while the meals for a 7kg cat assume that the cat is large framed rather than overweight.

Two meals for a 4kg cat
5% of body weight = 200 grams of food daily.
Morning meal (100g)
• 2 raw chicken necks
Afternoon meal (100g)
• raw lamb neck slice
• a few drops of fish oil
• a pinch of flax meal

Two meals for a 5kg cat
5% of body weight = 250 grams of food daily.
Morning meal (125g)
• 3 raw chicken necks
• contents of Vitamin E capsule
Afternoon meal (125g)
• tinned pilchards in tomato sauce
• mashed sweet potato and pumpkin
• a pinch of flax meal

Two meals for a 6kg cat
This cat is overweight, so should be fed 5% of its target weight of 5kg daily (200g).
Morning meal (100g)
- 1 raw chicken wing
- 1 raw egg yolk

Afternoon meal (100g)
- 20g soaked rolled quinoa mash
- 80g diced raw roo meat
- 1 tsp cod liver oil

Two meals for a 7kg cat
This cat is not a big eater and is fine with 3% of its body weight daily = 210 grams.
Morning meal (105g)
- 1 raw chicken neck
- 30g leftover lamb and vegetable stir-fry
- 45g raw whitebait

Afternoon meal (105g)
- 100g raw lamb mince
- 5g of plain yogurt

What not to give cats

Some drugs, herbs and foods cause dangerous reactions that cat owners should be aware of. The most important ones are:
- Paracetamol, contained in some pain-killing tablets, is highly poisonous to cats, so never give in any amount.

- Aspirin and herbs that reduce blood clotting should be avoided or used under veterinary supervision.
- High doses of the herb ginkgo biloba with fish oil can reduce blood clotting slightly, so stop the medication a few days prior to and after surgery.
- Alpha lipoic acid should be given to cats with care, or not at all.
- The herb marshmallow (sometimes combined with slippery elm bark powder for diarrhoea treatment) can increase blood sugar in diabetic cats, which can worsen their condition.

Some aromatherapy oils are poisonous to cats. Citronella, eucalyptus and tea tree oils should not be applied to the skin as they can be toxic even in small doses if licked off by the cat.

Some flowers, especially lilies (often in flower arrangements) can be highly toxic to cats, causing kidney failure.

Soy protein products may contribute to hyperthyroidism, allergy or autoimmunity in cats, so they are best avoided.[101] (The soy oil in which fish are often canned is likely to be fine as it does not contain soy protein.)

Over-vaccination can cause unnecessary health

problems for cats, so minimise vaccination to every three years or when needed according to blood test (see pages 59–62).

Reducing unnecessary vaccination and feeding a natural diet are the two most useful steps you can take in caring for your cat's health.

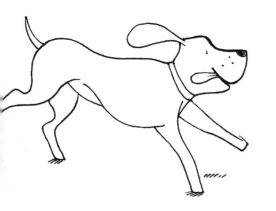

endnotes

1	Puotinen, C. Research on Wild Canids.
2	Schultze, K. *Natural Nutrition for Dogs and Cats*.
3	Kopellis McLeod, K. *105 Great Ideas to Having a Well Behaved Dog*.
4	Eliasens, Mogens. *Raw Food for Dogs*; Kopellis McLeod, K. *105 Great Ideas to Having a Well Behaved Dog*.
5	See Jan Fennell, *The Practical Dog Listener*.
6	Sjaastad, Hove and Sand. Physiology of Domestic Animals.
7	ibid.
8	ibid.
9	ibid.
10	ibid.
11	see www.ziwipeak.com for packet dog and cat food which is air dried and has no carbohydrate content.
12	Kasstrom, H. Nutrition, Weight gain and Development of Hip Dysplasia.
13	Costa, N. *A Short Supplement on the Nutrition of the Dog and Cat*.
14	Leggett, Daverick. A Guide to the Energetics of Food.
15	Sjaastad, Hove and Sand. Physiology of Domestic Animals.
16	ibid.
17	Murray, M. *The Healing Power of Herbs*; Sjaastad, Hove and Sand. Physiology of Domestic Animals; Wynn, S. Nutrients and Botanicals.
18	Short, K. *Quick Poison Slow Poison; A–Z of Chemicals in the Home*. To find safe products you can use in your home, see the Planet Ark shop in your capital city.

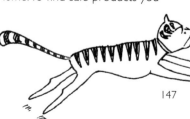

19   Sjaastad, Hove and Sand. Physiology of Domestic
        Animals; Puotinen, C. Research on Wild Canids.
20   Eliasens, Mogens. *Raw Food for Dogs.*
21   Eliasens, Mogens. *Raw Food for Dogs*; Kopellis
        McLeod, K. *105 Great Ideas to Having a Well
        Behaved Dog.*
22   Sjaastad, Hove and Sand. Physiology of Domestic
        Animals.
23   Eliasens, Mogens. *Raw Food for Dogs*; Kopellis
        McLeod, K. *105 Great Ideas to Having a Well
        Behaved Dog.*
24   Eliasens, Mogens. *Raw Food for Dogs*; www.
        greenpet.com.au, www.ntphealthproducts.com,
        and www.vetsallnatural.com.au all have good
        supplements.
25   Leggett, Daverick. A Guide to the Energetics of
        Food.
26   ibid.
27   ibid.
28   Metagenics seminar: see www.metagenics.com.
29   Linus Pauling Institute at the University of
        Oregon, USA http://lpi.oregonstate.edu/
30   ibid.
31   Coffarelli C. et al. Gastrointestinal Symptoms in
        Patients with Asthma; Metagenics seminar: see
        www.metagenics.com.
32   Sjaastad, Hove and Sand. Physiology of Domestic
        Animals.
33   Puotinen, C. Research on Wild Canids.
34   Eliasens, Mogens. *Raw Food for Dogs.*
35   Bovee, Kenneth C. *Mythology of Protein Restriction
        for Dogs.*
36   American Small Animal Hospital Vaccination
        Guidelines; Dodds, W.J. Vaccination Protocols.
37   ibid.
38   American Small Animal Hospital Vaccination
        Guidelines; Dodds, W.J. Vaccination Protocols;
        Short, K. *Quick Poison Slow Poison.*
39   Sjaastad, Hove and Sand. Physiology of Domestic
        Animals.
40   Short, K. *Quick Poison Slow Poison.*

41 ibid.
42 ibid.
43 Eliasens, Mogens. *Raw Food for Dogs*; Puotinen, C. Research on Wild Canids.
44 Available from distributors in most major cities and online at <www.drianbillinghurst.com/>.
45 Kasstrom, H. Nutrition, Weight gain and Development of Hip Dysplasia.
46 Sjaastad, Hove and Sand. Physiology of Domestic Animals.
47 Puotinen, C. Research on Wild Canids.
48 www.happysnax.com.au and www.vetsbest.com.au for good air-dried liver treats.
49 Short, K. *Quick Poison Slow Poison*.
50 Block, J. Clinical Evidence Supporting Cancer Risk Reduction; Osieki, Henry. *Cancer*.
51 Wray, A, Wray C. *Salmonellosis in Domestic Animals*.
52 Leggett, Daverick. A Guide to the Energetics of Food.
53 De Bairacli Levy, Juliette. *The Complete Herbal Handbook for the Dog and Cat*.
54 Block, J. Clinical Evidence Supporting Cancer Risk Reduction; Osieki, Henry. *Cancer*
55 Leggett, Daverick. A Guide to the Energetics of Food.
56 Puotinen, C. Research on Wild Canids.
57 Wynn, S. Nutrients and Botanicals.
58 Osieki, Henry. *Cancer*
59 Brigg, W. www.fulhealthindustries.com.au.
60 Block, J. Clinical Evidence Supporting Cancer Risk Reduction; Osieki, Henry. *Cancer*.
61 Bone, K. *A Clinical Guide to Blending Liquid Herbs*; Fougere, B. *The Pet Lover's Guide to Natural Healing*.
62 Murray, M. *The Healing Power of Herbs*.
63 *A–Z of Chemicals in the Home*; Short, K. *Quick Poison Slow Poison*.
64 Cabot S, Jasinska M. *Your Thyroid Problems Solved*.
65 *A–Z of Chemicals in the Home*; Short, K. *Quick Poison Slow Poison*.

66   Murray, M. *The Healing Power of Herbs.*

67   www.greenpet.com.au, www.ntphealthproducts.com, www.vetsallnatural.com.au all have good supplements to go with natural diets for dogs and cats.

68   Block, J. Clinical Evidence Supporting Cancer Risk Reduction; Osieki, Henry. *Cancer.*

69   ibid.

70   Block, J. Clinical Evidence Supporting Cancer Risk Reduction; Boelsma et al. Nutritional Skin Care; SanGiovanni J, Chew E. The Role of Omega-3.

71   www.greenpet.com.au, www.ntphealthproducts.com, and www.vetsallnatural.com.au.

72   ibid.

73   Linus Pauling Institute at the University of Oregon, USA http://lpi.oregonstate.edu/

74   Bioceuticals at www.bioceuticals.com.au for product information on the probiotic *Saccharomyces boulardii*; Protexin; www.iahp.com.au.

75   Coffarelli C. et al. Gastrointestinal Symptoms in Patients with Asthma; Metagenics seminar: see www.metagenics.com.

76   Bioceuticals at www.bioceuticals.com.au for product information on *Saccharomyces boulardii*; Metagenics seminar: see www.metagenics.com.

77   Linus Pauling Institute at the University of Oregon, USA http://lpi.oregonstate.edu/

78   *Pottenger's Cats.* This small book documents the research project comparing cats fed on raw v. cooked food (Price-Pottenger Nutrition Foundation Inc.).

79   Zoran D. The Carnivore Connection.

80   Sjaastad, Hove and Sand. Physiology of Domestic Animals; Wynn, S. Nutrients and Botanicals; Zoran D. The Carnivore Connection.

81   Wynn, S. Nutrients and Botanicals; Zoran D. The Carnivore Connection.

82   Sjaastad, Hove and Sand. Physiology of Domestic Animals; Zoran D. The Carnivore Connection.

83   Costa, N. *A Short Supplement on the Nutrition of the Dog and Cat*; Wynn, S. Nutrients and Botanicals; Zoran D. The Carnivore Connection;

R. Malik, Feeding Cats for health and Longevity.

84   Fitch H.M. and D.A. Fagan, Focal palatine erosion; Phillips, J.A. Bone Consumption by Cheetahs.

85   Wynn, S. Nutrients and Botanicals; Zoran D. The Carnivore Connection. Most of these subjects are covered by the references listed in this book. I can direct readers to individual papers if they wish to contact me.

86   Wynn, S. Nutrients and Botanicals; Zoran D. The Carnivore Connection.

87   ibid.

88   Zoran D. The Carnivore Connection.

89   Sjaastad, Hove and Sand. Physiology of Domestic Animals.

90   Short, K. *Quick Poison Slow Poison.*

91   www.ziwipeak.com for packet dog and cat food which is air-dried and has no carbohydrate content.

92   Billinghurst, Dr Ian. *Give Your Dog a Bone; Grow Your Pup With Bones; The BARF Diet.*

93   www.greenpet.com.au, www.ntphealthproducts.com, and www.vetsallnatural.com.au.

94   www.greenpet.com.au, www.ntphealthproducts.com, and www.vetsallnatural.com.au. These companies all have good supplements to go with natural diets for dogs and cats.

95   Zoran D. The Carnivore Connection.

96   Leggett, Daverick. A Guide to the Energetics of Food.

97   www.greenpet.com.au, www.ntphealthproducts.com, and www.vetsallnatural.com.au, www.happysnax.com.au and www.vetsbest.com.au for air-dried liver treats; www.ziwipeak.com for air-dried dog and cat food with no carbohydrate content.

98   www.ziwipeak.com for air-dried dog and cat food with no carbohydrate content.

99   Wynn, S. Nutrients and Botanicals; Zoran D. The Carnivore Connection.

100   www.greenpet.com.au, www.ntphealthproducts.com, and www.vetsallnatural.com.au.

101   White H. et al. Effect of Dietary Soy.

annotated bibliography

Billinghurst, Dr Ian. *Give Your Dog a Bone*, 1993, *Grow Your Pup With Bones*, 1998, *The BARF Diet*, 2001. Warrigal Publishing.

Block, J. Clinical Evidence Supporting Cancer Risk Reduction with Antioxidants and Implications for Diet and Supplementation. *J Am Nutr Assoc*, 3 (3), 2000.

Boelsma E, Hendriks H, Roza L. Nutritional Skin Care: health effects of micronutrients and fatty acids, *Am J Clin Nutr*, 2001, vol 73.

Bone, K. *A Clinical Guide to Blending Liquid Herbs*. Elsevier 2003.

Bone, K. *Principles and Practice of Phytotherapy*. Elsevier 2000.

Bovee, Kenneth C. *Mythology of Protein Restriction for Dogs with Reduced Renal Function*. Department of Clinical Studies, School of Veterinary Medicine, University of Pennsylvania, Philadelphia.

Brigg, W. www.fulhealthindustries.com.au

Coffarelli C. et al. Gastrointestinal Symptoms in Patients with Asthma. *Arch Dis Child*, Feb 2000, 82 (2).

———. Gastrointestinal Symptoms in Atopic Excema. *Arch Dis Child*, Mar 1998, 78 (3).

Cabot S, Jasinska M. *Your Thyroid Problems Solved*. WHAS 2006.

Costa, N. *A Short Supplement on the Nutrition of the Dog and Cat*. Murdoch University School of Veterinary Studies 1996.

De Bairacli Levy, Juliette. *The Complete Herbal Handbook for the Dog and Cat*. Faber & Faber. First published 1955. Juliette, a vet and dog breeder, is a world leader in natural diet and herbal treatment for dogs.

Dodds, WJ. Vaccination Protocols for Dogs Predisposed

to Vaccine Reactions. *J Am Anim Hosp Assoc,* May/June 2001.

——. Advocate for Serological Testing After Vaccination. *J Am Vet Med Assoc,* Jan 2003.

——. Assessing the Need for Booster Vaccination. *Can Vet J,* Feb 2002.

Eliasens, Mogens. *Raw Food for Dogs — the Ultimate Reference for Dog Owners.* This 340-page ebook is recommended for new puppy owners and dog breeders and can be bought for a reasonable price on the net <http://k9joy.com/RawFoodForDogs/index.php?camp=5234_campaign>
Some excellent articles on natural feeding are available free at this website. Mogens is a chemist and has also written books on the wolf's diet and on dog training, and runs an email chat site on natural dog care called 'The Peeing Post'. He has extensive experience with dogs as an army dog handler and trainer.

Fennell, J. *The Practical Dog Listener. The 30 day path to a lifelong understanding of your dog,* Harper Collins 2002.

Fitch H.M. and D.A. Fagan, 'Focal palatine erosion associated with Dental Malocclusion in Captive Cheetahs', *Zoo Biology* (1), 1982.

Fougere, B. *The Pet Lover's Guide to Natural Healing for Dogs and Cats.* Elsevier 2006.

Kasstrom, H. Nutrition, Weight gain and Development of Hip Dysplasia. An Experimental Investigation in Growing Dogs with Special Reference to the Effect of Feeding Intensity. *Acta Radio. Supp.* 1975.

Kasstrom, H, Kealy RD, Olsson SE, Monti KL, et al. Effects of Limited Food Consumption on the Incidence of Hip Dysplasia in Growing Dogs. *J Am Vet Med Assoc,* 1992.

Kopellis McLeod, K. *105 Great Ideas to Having a Well Behaved Dog.* A good, inexpensive book on dog training available from PO Box 627, Morley, WA 6943.

Leggett, Daverick. A Guide to the Energetics of Food based on the Traditions of Chinese Medicine 2005 (wall chart), also a work book by same author, both related to human health) at <www.redwingboks.com> (My colleague in Perth, Dr Bruce Ferguson of Murdoch University, is currently writing a book on veterinary TCM food therapy.)

Malik, R. 'Feeding Cats for health and Longevity', *The Veterinarian*, Nov 2007.

Metagenics seminar: Advances in the Management of Digestive and Allergic Disorders, Feb 2007. See www.metagenics.com

Murray, M. *The Healing Power of Herbs*. Prima 1995.

Osieki, Henry. *Cancer: A Nutritional/Biochemical Approach*. Bioconcepts Publishing 2002. Osieki has also written a very useful reference book which lists nutritional supplements for different disease conditions, *The Physician's Handbook of Clinical Nutrition*, Bioconcepts Publishing 1998.

Phillips, F. *The Alternative Cat*. Duffy & Snellgrove 1998. Dr Fiona Phillips is a holistic veterinarian from NSW with a degree in nutrition. An informative and fun book.

Phillips, J.A. 'Bone Consumption by Cheetahs at undisturbed kills', *J. of Mammalogy* 74 (2), 1993.

Pottenger, F.M. *Pottenger's Cats – a study in nutrition*, Price-Pottenger Nutrition Foundation, www.ppnf.org/catalog/

Puotinen, C. Research on Wild Canids Can Help Inform Dietary Planning for Dogs. *The Whole Dog Journal*, March 2005.

SanGiovanni, J. and Chew, E. The Role of Omega-3 long chain fatty acids in health and disease of the retina. *Prog Retina Eye Res*, Jan 2005, 24 (1).

Schultze, K. *Natural Nutrition for Dogs and Cats*. Hay House USA 1998 (a good small book — order in Australia from www.hayhouse.com.au).

Short, K. *Quick Poison Slow Poison — Pesticide Risk in the*

Lucky Country. Southwood Press 1994.

Sjaastad, Hove and Sand. Physiology of Domestic Animals. *Scandinavian Veterinary Press* 2004.

Williams, E. FeedWell 2008. See www.vividpublishing. com.au/feedwell

Wray, A. and Wray, C. *Salmonellosis in Domestic Animals.* CABI Publishing 2000.

Wright, M. *The Healthy Cat.* 1998, Grass Roots magazine publishing.

Wynn, S. Nutrients and Botanicals in the treatment of Diabetes Mellitus in Veterinary Practice. *Alt Vet Med,* Sept 2001.

White, H. et al. Effect of Dietary Soy on Serum Thyroid Concentrations in Healthy Cats. *Am J of Vet Res,* 2004, 85 (5).

Zoran, D. The Carnivore Connection to Nutrition in Cats. *JAVMA,* 2002, 221 (11).

acknowledgements

I owe much of what I have learned to my trusting clients and their beloved animals, as well as my husband Garry and our children Katey and Isaac, who have travelled with me along my path of discovery by allowing me to treat them!

I would like to thank Garry for all the late night formatting work, and to Donalea Patman for her finetuning of the format in the original edition. Special thanks to my sister Kate Kenny and brother Lawrie Horner for proofreading, and to all the readers of earlier drafts of the book — Rosemary Hood, Bruce Ferguson, Ian Billinghurst, Suzanne Dewar, Eva Hart, Jill Shaw, Anne Perryer and Kerry Avanell. Each reader suggested unique and important changes that helped change this book for the better. Thank you to Janet Blagg for her further diligent and creative rearrangement of my writing, and to all the other staff at Fremantle Press for this third edition, and for launching this book into the public domain. I especially thank Dr Rosemary Hood from Animal Nurture, whose honest and open discussions helped me to organise my thoughts for this book and bring it into existence in the first place.

I have gained much inspiration over many years from my holistic colleagues in Australia and overseas, practitioners who dare to investigate outside the square and treat their patients in ways I think the animals might choose for themselves.

which veg do I cook?

Do cats need veg a fruit?

Shampoo.

Inflammatory Bowel

1/2 tablespoon   2 parts marshmallow
                              root
                  1 part slippery elm
                  1 part plantain leaf
                  1 part licorice root.

psyllium husk. FOS frutooligosacchari

eat burpees.

feed Nestle once a day
      Cat manytimes?
which fish oil to get for cat
a dog?

Weight kg 72.9 - 64.5 = 8.4 kg.
  20-30 per wk. = 8400 grams
              × 20% = 1680 ÷ 6
                    = 280 grams
                      a day.